GW01086771

LIVING
WORDS

THE WORDS OF CHRIST IN ARAMAIC - ENGLISH INTERLINEAR EDITION

Illustrated with Christian symbols

Edited by
Joseph Elias

2003

Living Words:
The Words of Christ in Aramaic-English Interlinear Edition

Copyright © 2002 Joseph P. Elias
All rights reserved.

This publication includes images from CorelDraw ® 8 & which are protected by the copyright laws of the U.S, Canada and elsewhere. Used under license.
It also includes images taken from ARION PRESS publication *Christian Symbols,* drawn by Rudolf Koch which may be used without permission.

Universal Publishers/uPUBLISH.com
USA * 2002

ISBN: 1-58112-604-2

www.uPUBLISH.com/books/elias.htm

INTRODUCTION

The purpose of this publication is to give an opportunity to a non-scholar to enjoy the sound of Christ's native Aramaic language, and at the same time to experience the healing power of his words.

The Jewish nation adopted Aramaic language during their captivity in Babylon and pushed out the use of ancient Hebrew in daily life. Aramaic was the language, in which Christ delivered his teaching to the ordinary people of Galilee, Judea and Samaria. We can safely presume that the first written records of Christ's words and parables, so called *logia,* were circled in Aramaic, though they have been lost.

The Greek gospels, which we presently have, simply translate Christ's Aramaic words into common Greek which was spoken in Greek colonies of Asia Minor, but was a foreign tongue to the apostles, yet a handy tool for spreading Good News to the pagan world.

It has been more than a century since a German scholar Gustav Dalman investigated the mother tongue of Jesus. He wrote a few books on Aramaic languages and their dialects, including the Galilean Aramaic. Since then a great deal of research has been done, but for the majority of people these achievements are out of reach.

For one thing, the ancient translations of the scriptures into Aramaic, so-called targums of Onkelos and Jonathan, including the Aramaic portions of Dead Sea scrolls and various translations into the ancient Syriac, which is a branch of the Aramaic family of languages, are being only recently fully researched.

On the other hand, Syriac documents use a variety of scripts and different notations for the vowels which fact creates a great difficulty to a non-specialist in this field. Recently, George Kiraz of the Syriac Institute has done a great job in editing and comparing ancient Syriac translations of the gospels and computerizing all data which will pave the way for further research.

The Aramaic transcription in English alphabet adopted in this edition should approximate the Aramaic pronunciation and give the reader an experience of hearing Christ speaking in his native language. The Aramaic text is based on the Peshitta translation of the gospels which has been widely used and adopted by eastern Christian churches since the fourth century, and in the opinion of many scholars comes closest to the native dialect of Christ.

A quite few changes in the Aramaic language occurred during first four centuries of the Christian era, and the Peshitta translation reflects these changes in vocabulary and grammar. Though following Peshitta text closely, I had to take into account some of the changes: I kept the Aramaic imperfect formant *y* for the third person instead of the Syriac *n*, the first singular pronoun *ana* instead of *ena*. I also replaced *kena, kenuta*, the imperfect *nettel, and* some of the Greek borrowings, like *namosa* and *diatheqe* with Aramaic equivalents.

The English translation follows the Aramaic text as closely as possible, even sometimes at the expense of literary English word order to make parallel reading easier to follow. I chose simpler English words to reflect the simple language of the original Greek *koine* and the Aramaic *peshitta* which both mean simple people's language.

The words of Christ are presented in a historical sequence, following the synopsis of the four gospels. The Sermon of the Mount and the Sermon of the Plain are quoted separately, thus giving fuller treatment to the passages of Luke on the assumption that these sermons were delivered more than once with similar phrases. The same holds true in the case of some similar parables which have minor variations, like the parable of minas and the parable of talents, also the parables of the great dinner and of the wedding banquet.

The title of the publication *Living Words* has two connotations. First, it is a representation of the living speech of Christ. To be able to pronounce and recite his words in his native language should give one an exciting experience, similar to listening to a recital of the Homeric poems in original Greek or chanting of ancient Sanskrit Vedas.

Living Words also could mean *life-giving* words. The words of Christ have their own power of changing people's mind and cleansing one's soul, same way as it happened in his days on earth. If you believe them and accept them as true, you have achieved your life's mission.

Christ's words are strong medications — they shouldn't be read all in one day — one page a day should be the right prescription. They should be read on a regular basis, like any other medication one may take. The main difference between our prescription medication and the *Living Words* is that Words' healing power is hundred percent guaranteed and there are no bills to be paid.

ARAMAIC LANGUAGE

The Aramaic language has the same features of all Semitic tongues - the main idea of a word is expressed in three or two consonants, all other grammatical functions use a combination of prefixes, suffixes and vowel changes.
The following list summarizes the more important terms:

PREFIXES

b- in, at, with	**d-** of, that, which, who
l- to, for	**w-** and

POSSESSIVE SUFFIXES

-i my	**-an** our
-ak your m	**-kon** your mpl
-ik your f	**-ken** your fpl
-eh his	**-hon** their m
-ah her	**-hen** their f

PERSONAL PRONOUNS

hu he	**hennon** they m
hi she	**hennen** they f
att you m	**atton** you mpl
atti you f	**atten** you fpl
ana I	**naxnan, xnan** we

DEMONSTRATIVES

hana this m	**halen** these m
hade this f	**halen** these f
haw that	**hanon** those m
hay that f	**hanen** those f

COPULAS

-u -w he is	**-ennon** they are m
-i -y she is	**-ennen** they are f
-att you are m	**-tton** you are mpl
-att you are f	**-tten** you are fpl
-na I am	**-nan** we are

PARTICLES

la not, no	**ger den** but
ma what	**man** who
ap also	**min** from, out of
'ad till, up to	**'am** with
lmana why	**aw** or
it there is/are	**lait** there is/are not
in if	**apla** neither
haSa now	**tub** again
rab great, big	**aikanna** as
kad when, while	**hakanna** thus, so

ARAMAIC TRANSCRIPTION AND PRONUNCIATION

CONSONANTS

'	alaf:	glottal stop, not pronounced, indicates vowel **a, e**
b	bet:	like **b** in 'boy', after a vowel like **v** or **w**
g	gamal	like **g** in 'get', after a vowel aspirated **gh**
d	dalat:	like a **d** in 'dad', after a vowel like **th** in 'then'
h	het:	like **h** in 'have'
w	waw:	a glide like **w** in 'wood', indicates vowel **o, u**
z	zayn:	like **z** in 'zoo'
x	xet:	pure breathing sound of **h** in the throat
T	thet:	velar emphatic **t** in the back throat
y	yod:	a glide like **y** in 'yes', indicates vowel **i, e**
k	kaf:	like **k** in 'kid', after a vowel and final like **kh**
l	lamad:	like **l** in 'leave'
m	mim:	like **m** in 'milk'
n	nun:	like **n** in 'no'
s	semkat:	like **s** in 'sit'
'	'e:	fricative sound or a gag in the throat
p	pe:	like **p** in 'pay', after a vowel like **f**
c	tsade:	like **ts** in 'tsar' or 'sits'
q	qof:	velar **k** in the back throat
r	resh:	rolled **r** like in Spanish
S	shin:	like **sh** in 'she'
t	taw:	like **t** in 'time', after a vowel aspirated like **th** in 'thin'

VOWELS

a long indicated by alaf, between **a** and **o**; short like **a** in 'mama'
e short **e** vowel like **e** in 'bed' or long like **ey** in final syllable or when indicated by yod
i long **i** like in 'see', mostly indicated by yod
o short or long **o**, like in 'gone', long indicated by waw
u like **u** in 'wood', long like **oo** in 'moon' indicated by waw
schwa short **e** sound between two or three consonants

ASPIRATION

The consonant stops **b, g, d, k, p, t,** so called *begadkepat,* when preceded by a vowel are aspirated and pronounced correspondingly as **v, gh, dh, kh, f, th.**
These stops become spirant consonants even across the word boundaries when preceded by any vowel. There is no aspiration if these stops are doubled or preceded by a consonant.

The child Jesus to his parents

L2,49

['Your father and I have been searching for you in great anxiety.']
mana ba'ein waiton li?
Why were you searching for me?
la yad'in atton dbeit abi wale li dehwe?
Did you not know that I must be in my Father's house?

To John the Baptist

Mt3,15

[John: 'I need to be baptized by you, and do you come to me?']
Sboq haSa: hakanna ger ya'e lan danmalle kullah zaddiquta.
Allow it now, for this way it becomes us to fulfill all justice.

The temptations - to the Satan

Mt4,4-10 L4,4-12

ktib: dla wa blaxma balxod xaiye barnaSa
It is written: 'Not on bread alone lives a human being.
ella bkoll milla dnapqa min pumeh dalaha.
but on every word that comes from the mouth of God.'
tub ktib: dla tnasse Imarya alahak.
Again it is written: 'You shall not tempt the Lord, your God.'
zel lak saTana!
Go away, Satan!
ktib ger: dalmarya alahak tisgod
Again it is written: 'Lord, your God, shall you worship
uleh balxodawhi tiplox.
and him alone shall you serve.'

The Good News

M1,14 Mt4,17

Slem leh zabna wamTat malkuta dalaha.
The time is fulfilled, and the kingdom of God has arrived.
tubu whaimenu basbarta!
Repent and believe the gospel!
tubu qerbat ger malkuta daSmaiya!
Repent, for the kingdom of heaven is at hand!

To his first followers

J1,38-43

mana ba'ein atton?
What are you looking for?
tau wtexzon!
Come, and you will see!
ta batari!
Come after me!

9

To Simon and Andrew
L5,4-10 Mt4,19 M1,17

dbar l'umqa warmau mcidtkon lcaida:
Lead into the deep and cast your nets for a catch!
la tidxal: min haSa bnainaSa tihwe ca'ed lxaiye.
Do not fear, from now on you will be catching men for life.
att hu Sim'on breh dyona att tiqre kepa:
You are Simon, the son of John, you will be called Kephas.
tau batari we'bedkon dtihwon caiyade dabnainaSa:
Come after me, and I will make you become fishers of men!

To Nathanael
J1,43

ha Sarrira'it bar israyel dnikla lait beh.
Behold, a true son of Israel, in whom there is no deceit.
'ad la iqreik pilippos: kad txet tetta att xazeitak.
Before Philip called you, I saw you under the fig tree.
'al dimret lak daxazeitak txet tetta att mhaimen att:
Because I told you that I saw you under the fig tree, you believe;
drawrban min halen texze.
you will see greater things than these.
amen amen amar-na lkon dtexzon Smaiya daptixin
Truly, truly I tell you, you will see the heavens opened and
wmalakawhi dalaha kad salqin wnaxtin lwat breh dnaSa.
the angels of God ascending and descending on the Son of man.

The wedding at Cana
J2,4-8

ma li wleki attta?
What is it to me and to you, woman?
la 'adakkel ettat Sa'ati.
My hour has not yet come.
mlau innen maiya laggane!
Fill the jars with water!
zlo'u mikkel waittau lreS smaka!
Draw some out now and take it to the headwaiter!

Cleansing of the temple
J2,16

Sqolu halen mikka!
Take these things out of here!
wla te'bduneh lbaiteh dabi beit tegurta!
And do not make my Father's house a marketplace!
storu haikla hana wlatlata yawmin ana aqim-na leh.
Destroy this temple, and in three days I will raise it up.

To Nicodemus - New birth

J3,3-18

amen amen amar-na lak din naS la mitiled min dreS
Truly, truly I say to you, unless one is born again
la miSkax dyexze malkuteh dalaha.
he cannot see the kingdom of God.
amen amen amar-na lak:
Truly, truly I tell you,
din naS la mitiled min maiya wruxa
unless one is born of water and the Spirit
la miSkax dye"ol lmalkuta dalaha.
he cannot enter into the kingdom of God.
middem dilid min bisra bisra-w
What is born of flesh is flesh
wmiddem dilid min ruxa ruxa-w.
and what is born of Spirit is Spirit.
la titdammar demret lak:
Do not be amazed that I told you:
dwale lkon lmitiladu min dreS.
You must be born again.
ruxa attar dcabya naSba wqalah Sama' att:
The wind where it wishes blows and you hear sound of it,
ella la yada' att aimikka atya wlaika aza:
but you do not know where it comes from or where it goes,
hakanna itawhi kollnaS dilid min ruxa.
so is everyone who is born of the Spirit.
att hu mallpaneh disrayel whalen la yada' att?
You are the teacher of Israel and you do not know this?
amen amen amar-na lak
Truly, truly I say to you,
dmiddem yad'in-nan mmallin-nan
that of what we know we speak
wmiddem daxazain mashadinan
and to what we have seen we testify
wsahaddutan la mqabblin-tton.
and our testimony you do not accept.
in dbar'a imret lkon wla mhaimnin-tton
If I tell you about the earthly things and you do not believe,
aikanna in emar dbaSmaiya thaimnunani?
how will you believe if I tell you about heavenly things?
wla naS sleq laSmaiya
No one has ascended into heaven,
ella haw danxet min Smaiya
but he who descended from heaven,
breh dnaSa haw ditawhi baSmaiya.
the Son of man, who is in heaven.

11

waikanna darim muSe xewya bmadbra
And as just as Moses lifted up the serpent in the desert,
hakanna 'atid lmittramu breh dnaSa
so must the Son of man be lifted up,
dkollnaS damhaimen beh la yebad
that whoever believes in him may not perish,
ella ihwon leh xaiye dal'alam.
but may have eternal life.
hakanna ger axxeb alaha l'alma
For God so loved the world
aikanna dlabreh ixidaya inten
that he gave his only begotten Son,
dkollman damhaimen beh la yebad
so that everyone who believes in him may not perish
ella ihwon leh xaiye dal'alam.
but may have eternal life.
la ger Saddar alaha labreh l'alma
For God did not send his Son to the world
daiduniwhi l'alma
to condemn the world,
ella dixxe 'alma bideh.
but that the world might be saved through him.
man damhaimen beh la mitdin
Whoever believes in him is not condemned,
wman dla mhaimen min kaddu din-u
he whoever does not believe has been condemned already,
dla mhaimen
because he has not believed
baSmeh dixidaya breh dalaha.
in the name of the only begotten Son of God.

The light and the darkness

J3,19-21

hana-w dina dnuhara etta l'alma
This is the judgment that the light has come into the world
waxxebu bnainaSa lxeSSoka yattir min dalnuhara:
and men loved the darkness rather than the light,
itaihon wau ger 'abadaihon biSe.
for their deeds were evil.
koll ger dsanyata 'abed sane lnuhara
For everyone who does evil hates the light
wla ate lwat nuhara:
and does not come toward the light,
dla itkassun 'abadawhi.
so that his deeds might not be exposed.

12

haw den d'abed Srara ate lwat nuhara
But whoever does the truth comes to the light
dityad'un 'abadawhi dbalaha 'abidin.
so that his deeds may be known as done in God.

The woman of Samaria

J4,7-26

habi li maiya eSte!
Give me water to drink!
illu yada' waiti mawhabta dalaha wmannu hana demar leki:
If you knew the gift of God and who it is who says to you:
habi li eSte: atti Sala waiti leh
'Give me a drink,' you would have asked him
wyaheb wa leki maiya xaiye.
and he would have given you living water.
koll diSte min halen maiya tub iche
Everyone who drinks of this water will thirst again,
koll den diSte min maiya dana etten leh la iche l'alam
but whoever drinks of water I will give him will never thirst,
ella maiya hanon dyaheb-na leh ihwon beh
but the water that I will give him will become in him
m'ina dmaiya dnab'in lxaiye dal'alam.
a well of water springing up to eternal life.
zeli qrai lba'aleki wtai lharka.
Go, call your husband and come here.
Sappir emarti: dlait li ba'ala
You are right in saying: I have no husband,
xammSa ger ba'alin hawau leki whana dit leki haSa
for five husbands you have had, and this one you now have
la wa ba'alek: hade Sarrirta emarti.
is not your husband, this you have said truly.
attta haimnini datya Sa'ta
Woman, believe me, an hour is coming
dla bhana Tura apla boriSlem
when neither on this mountain nor in Jerusalem
tisgdun laba.
will you worship the Father.
atton sagdin-tton lmiddem la yad'in-tton
You worship what you do not know,
xanan den sagdin-nan lma dyad'in-nan
we worship what we know,
dxaiye min yudaye innon.
For salvation is from the Jews.
ella atya Sa'ta whaSa iteh emmati dsagode Sarrire
But an hour is coming and now is, when the true worshippers

13

sigdun laba bruxa wbaSrara.
will worship the Father in spirit and truth.
ap aba ger dak halen sagode ba'e.
for also the Father seeks such worshippers.
ruxa-w ger alaha wailen dsagdin leh
God is spirit, and those who worship him,
bruxa wabSrara wale disgdun.
in spirit and truth must worship.
ana-na dammallel-na 'ammeki.
I am he, the one who is speaking with you.

The harvest
J4,32-38

it li mekulta dekol aida datton la yad'in-tton.
I have food to eat that you do not know about.
mekulti dili iteh de'bbed cibyaneh dman dSaddrani
My food is to do the will of him who sent me
weSalmiwhi la'abadeh.
and to accomplish his work.
la atton amrin: dbatar arb'a yarxin ate xacada?
Do you not say: After four months comes the harvest?
ha amar-na Ikon: darimu 'ainaikon wxazau ar'ata
Look up, I say to you, raise your eyes and look at the fields,
daxawwar wmaTTi laxacada min kaddu.
that they are white and ripe for harvest already.
waina dxaced arga naseb wkanneS pere
And he who reaps receives wages and gathers fruit
lxaiye dal'alam: wzaro'a wxacoda
for life eternal, so that the sower and the reaper
akda yexdun.
together may rejoice.
bhade ger iteh millta daSrara: daxren-u zara' waxren xaced.
For here the sayings holds true:'One sows and another reaps.'
ana Saddartkon lmexcad middem dla wa atton litton beh
I sent you to reap for which you have not labored,
xrane ger liyu watton 'alton 'al 'amilhon dhanon.
others toiled and you entered into their labor.

Healing an official's son
J4,46-54
in atwata wtidmerata la texzon la thaimnun.
Unless you see miracles and wonders, you do not believe.
zel brak xaiy-u.
Go, your son lives!

14

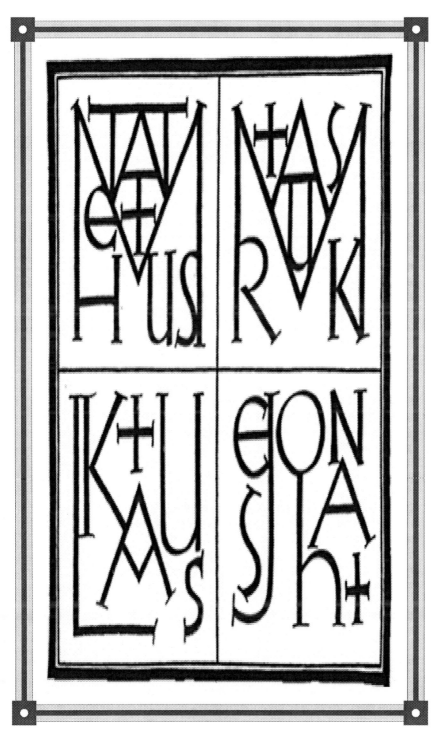

15

The cure of the demoniac

M1,25 L4,35

skor pumak wpoq minneh!
Shut your mouth and come out of him!

Unwelcome in Nazareth

L4,18-27

ruxeh dmarya 'alai wmiTTol hana maSxani
'The Spirit of the Lord is upon me, because he had anointed me
lamsabbaru lmiskene
to preach good news to the poor.
wSalxani lmassayu latbirai libba
He has sent me to heal the brokenhearted
walmakrazu laSbaiya Subqana
and to preach to the captives forgiveness
wla'awire xazaya
and to the blind sight
lamSararu latbire bSubqana
and to free those oppressed with forgiveness
walmakrazu Satta mqabalta lmarya.
and to preach the year acceptable to the Lord.'
dyawmana iStallam ktaba hana bidnaikon.
Today this scripture has been fulfilled in your ears.
kbar temrun li matla hana: asya assa napSak.
Surely, you will tell me this proverb: 'Doctor, cure yourself.
wkoll daSma'an da'abadt bakpar naxom
What we have heard you did at Capernaum
'abed ap harka bamdittak.
do also here in your hometown.'
amen amar-na lkon dlait nbiyya dmitqabbal bamditteh.
Truly I tell you, no prophet is welcome in his hometown.
Srara ger amar-na lkon dsaggi armlata it wai beit israyel
But in truth I tell you there were many widows in Israel
byawmai eliyya kad ittxedu Smaiya Snin tlat
in the days of Elias when the sky was closed for three years
wyarxe Sta wahwa kapna rabba bkullah ar'a
and six months, when there was a great famine over all the land,
wallet xada minnhen la iStaddar eliyya
and to none of these was sent Elias
ella lcarpat dcaidan lwat attta armalta.
but only to Zarephath of Sidon to a woman, a widow.
wsaggiye garbe it wau beit israyel byawmai eliSa
And there were many lepers in Israel in the days of Elisha
wxad minnhon itdakki ella in na'aman aramaya.
and none of them was cleansed except Naaman the Syrian.

Preaching the gospel

M1,38

halleku lqurya wlamdinata!
Let us go to the villages and towns!
dap lamdinata xranyata wale li lamsabbaru
Also to the other towns I must preach
malkuteh dalaha d'al hade iStaddret.
the kingdom of God, because for this I was sent.

The leper

M1,41 Mt8,3 L5,13

cabe-na itdakka!
I am willing, be cleansed!
xazi lma lnaS amar att
See that you tell no one;
ella zel xawwa napSak lkahane
but go, show yourself to the priest and
wqarreb qurbana ak dpaqqed muSe lasahaduthon.
make an offering what Moses commanded as a proof to them.

The healing of the paralytic

Mt9,2 L5,20

itlabbab beri Sbiqin lak xaTahain!
Take courage, my son, your sins are forgiven you!
mana mitxaSSbin-tton biSata blibbkon?
Why do you think evil in your hearts?
mana ger pSiq lmemar daSbiqin lak xaTahain
For what is easier, to say that your sins are forgiven you
aw lmemar: qum hallek?
or to say, arise and walk?
dtidd'un den dSulTana it labreh dnaSa bar'a
But that you may know that the Son of man has power on earth
lmiSbaq xaTahe:
to forgive sins:
qum Sqol 'arsak wzel lbaitak.
'Rise, take up your bed and go to your home!'

Mercy

Mt9,12

la sniqin xalime 'al asya ella ailen dbiSa'it 'abidin.
Not the healthy need the doctor, but those who get sick.
zelu illapu manau: xanana ba'e wla debexta
Go learn what this means: 'I desire mercy, not sacrifice,'
la ger etteit deqre lzaddiqe ella lxaTTaye.
for I did not come to call on the just but on the sinners.

17

About fasting - the old and new wine

dalma miSkxin bnawhi dagnona lamcam
Can the wedding guests fast
kma dxatna 'ammhon?
as long as the bridegroom is with them?
atein den yawmata
But the days are coming
kad iStqel minnhon xatna
when the bridegroom will be taken from them,
whaiden icumun.
then they will fast.
la naS rame urqa'ta xdatta 'al mana blaya
No one places a new patch on an worn-out garment,
dla tittop malyutah min haw naxta
lest its seams should tear away from that garment
wihwe biz'a yattira.
and the hole become larger.
wla ramein xamra xadta bziqqe blayata
And they do not put new wine into worn-out wineskins,
dla micTarin ziqqe wxamra miteSed
lest the skins should rip and wine pour out
wziqqe abdan:
and the wineskins be ruined
ella ramein xamra xadta bziqqe xadtata
but they put new wine into new wineskins
watraihon mitnaTrin.
and both are preserved.
wla naS Sate xamra 'attiqa wmixda ba'e xadta
And no one after drinking old wine desires right away new,
amar ger: 'attiqa bassim.
for he says: 'The old is good.'

The Lord of the Sabbath

Mt12,3-8 M2,25-28 L6,3-5

la qraiton mana 'abad dawid kad kpen
Have you not read what David did when he was hungry
wailen d'ammeh?
and those who were with him?
aikanna 'al lbaita dalaha
how he entered the house of God
wlaxma dpatoreh dmarya ekal
and ate the bread of the Lord's table

18

haw dla SalliT wa leh lmekal wla lailen d'ammeh
which was not lawful for him to eat nor for those with him,
ella in lkahane balxod.
but for priests only.
aw la qraiton boraita dkahane bhaikla
or have you not read in the law that the priests in the temple
maxalin lah lSabbta wadla 'edlai innon
disregard the Sabbath and are without the blame?
amar-na lkon den drabb min haikla it harka.
But I say to you that someone greater than the temple is here.
illu den yad'in waiton manau:
But if only you knew what it means:
xanana cabe-na wla debexta:
'I desire mercy and not sacrifice,'
la mxaiybin waiton lailen dadla 'edlai innon.
you would not condemn those who are blameless.
dSabbta miTTol barnaSa itbaryat:
The Sabbath was made for man,
wla wa barnaSa miTTol Sabbta:
and not man for the Sabbath.
marah-u hakel wap dSabbta breh dnaSa.
So the lord even of the Sabbath is the Son of man.

The man with the withered hand
Mt12,11 M3,3 L6,8
eSa'elkon mana SalliT bSabbta
I ask you, is it lawful on the Sabbath
lme'bbad dTab aw dbiS
to do good or to do evil,
napSa lmaxxayu aw lmawbadu?
to save life or to destroy it?
mannu minnkon gabra dit leh 'irba xad
Who among you men that has one sheep
win napel bxabbara
and it falls into a pit
byawma dSabbta la axed wamqim leh?
on the day of Sabbath, would not grab it and raise it out?
kma den yattir barnaSa min 'irba.
Now how much more important is a man than a sheep.
maden SaliT-u bSabbta lme'bbad dSappir.
So then it is lawful on the Sabbath to do good.
qum ta lak lmec'at knuSta!
Come and stand in the middle of the congregation!
pSoT idak!
Stretch out your hand!

19

THE BEATITUDES   *Mt5,3-12*

Tubaihon lmiskene brux ddilhon-i malkuta daSmaiya.
Blessed are the poor in spirit, for theirs is the kingdom of heaven.
Tubaihon labile dhinnon itbayun.
Blessed are those who mourn, for they will be comforted.
Tubaihon lmakkike dhinnon yertun ar'a.
Blessed are the meek, for they will inherit the earth.
Tubaihon lailen dkapnin wachein Izaddiquta
Blessed are those who hunger and thirst for justice,
dhinnon isibb'un.
for they will be satisfied.
Tubaihon lamraxmane da'alaihon ihwon raxme.
Blessed are the merciful, for upon them will be mercies.
Tubaihon lailen dadkein blibbhon
Blessed are those who are pure in their heart,
dhinnon ixzon lalaha.
for they will see God.
Tubaihon 'abdai Slama dabnawhi dalaha itiqron.
Blessed are the peacemakers, for they will be called sons of God.
Tubaihon lailen ditirdepu miTTol zaddiquta
Blessed are those who are persecuted because of righteousness,
ddilhon malkuta daSmaiya.
for theirs is the kingdom of heaven.
Tubaikon emmati damxassdin lkon wradpin lkon
Blessed you are when they curse you and persecute you
wamrin 'alaikon koll milla biSa miTTolati bdaggaluta.
and say about you every evil word because of me falsely.
haiden xadau warwazu dagrakon sggi baSmaiya
Then rejoice and be glad, for your reward is great in heaven.
hakanna ger rdapu lanbiyye dmin qdamaikon.
So they persecuted the prophets who were before you.

The salt of the earth
     Mt5,13

atton innon milxah dar'a.
You are the salt of the earth.
inhu den dmilxa tipkah bmana titemlax?
but if the salt should go flat, with what will it be salted?
lmiddem la aza ella dtiStde lbar
It is fit for nothing, but to be thrown outside
wtitdiS min naSa.
and trampled by men.

The light of the world

Mt5, 14-16

atton nuhareh d'alma.
You are the light of the world.
la miSkxa dtiTSe mditta d'al Tura banya.
It is not possible to hide a city built on a mountain.
wla manihrin Sraga wsaimin leh txet sata.
And they do not light a lamp and place it under the basket,
ella 'al mnarta wmanhar lkoll ailen dabbaita innon.
but upon its stand and it gives light to all those in the house.
hakanna inhar nuhirkon qdam bnainaSa:
So let your light shine before men,
dyexzon 'abadaikon Tabe
that they may see your good works
waiSabbxun labukon dbaSmaiya.
and glorify your Father who is in heaven.

On the law and the prophets

Mt5, 17-20

la tisibbrun detteit deSre oraita aw nbiyye:
Do not think that I came to destroy the law or the prophets,
la etteit deSre ella demalle.
I came not to destroy but to fulfill.
amen ger amar-na lkon da'adamma dye'brun Smaiya war'a
For truly I say to you, till heaven and earth pass away,
yod xada aw xad sirTa la ye'bar min oraita
one iota or one stroke will not pass from the law
'adamma dkoll ihwe.
until everything happens.
koll man hakel diSre xad min puqdane halen z'ore
All who shall break one of these small commandments,
wyallep hakanna labnainaSa
and shall teach men so,
bcira itiqre bmalkuta daSmaiya.
will be called little in the kingdom of heaven.
koll den dye'bbed wyallep hana
but all who will do and teach this,
rabba itiqre bmalkuta daSmaiya.
shall be called great in the kingdom of heaven.
amar-na lkon ger din la tettar zaddiquton
For I say to you that unless your justice exceeds
yattir min dsapre wapriSe
more than that of scribes and Pharisees
la te"lun lmalkuta daSmaiya.
you will not enter the kingdom of heaven.

On murder and wrath

Mt5,21-26

Sma'ton ditamar lqadmaye:
You have heard that was said to those before:
la tiqTol wkoll diqTol mxaiyab Idina.
'You shall not kill and all whoever kills shall be liable to judgment.'
ana den amar-na Ikon dkoll man dirgaz 'al axuhi iqe
But I say to you, whoever is angry with his brother in vain
mxaiyab-u Idina.
will be liable to judgment.
wkoll dyemar laxuhi raqa
And whoever says to his brother 'I spit',
mxaiyab-u IknuSta.
will be liable to the council.
wkoll dman dyemar lella mxaiyab Igehanna dnura.
and whoever says 'you stupid' will be liable to hell of fire.
inhu hakel damqarreb att qurbanak 'al madbxa wtamman
If you, therefore, offer your gift at the altar and there
titdakar daxid 'alaik axuk akta middem
you should remember that your brother holds a grudge against you,
Sboq tamman qurbanak 'al madbxa wzel luqdam etra'a
leave there your gift at the altar and go first to be reconciled
'am axuk whaiden ta qarreb qurbanak.
to your brother and then come offer your gift.
hawait mit'awe 'am b'eldinak 'agal
Reconcile with your opponent at law quickly,
'ad 'ammeh att burxa
while you are with him on the way,
dalma b'eldinak yaSilmak Idaiyana
or your accuser may hand you over to the judge and
wdaiyana yaSilmak Igabaya wtippel beit 'assire.
the judge hand you over to the guard and you may be put in prison.
wamen amar-na lak dla tippoq min tamman
And truly I say to you, you will not get out of there
'adamma dditten Samona xraiya.
until you have paid the last penny.

On adultery and divorce

Mt5,27-32

Sma'ton ditamar: dla tgur.
You have heard that it was said: 'You shall not commit adultery.'
ana den amar-na Ikon dkoll man dxaze attta ak dirgih
But I say to you that everyone who looks at a woman lustfully
mixda garah blibbeh.
has already committed adultery in his heart.

23

in den 'ainak dyammina makiSla lak xacih waSdih minnak:
For if your right eye offends you pluck it out and throw it from you,
paqqax lak ger dyebad xad haddamak
for it is better for you that one of your members should perish
wla kulleh pagrak ippel begehanna.
than that your whole body should fall into hell.
win idak dyammina makiSla lak psoq Sdih minnak:
And if your right hand offends you cut it off and throw it from you,
paqqax lak ger dyebad xad min haddamak
for it is better that one of your members should perish
wla kullah pagrak ippel bgehanna.
than that your whole body should fall into hell.
itamar: dman dSare attteh
It has been said: 'Whoever divorces his wife
itten lah ktaba ddulala.
should give her a writing of divorce.'
ana den amar-na Ikon dkoll man dSare attteh
But I say to you, whoever divorces his wife,
Ibar min millta dzanyuta 'abed lah datgur
except the case of fornication, makes her commit adultery,
wman dSaqel Sbiqta ga'ar.
and he who takes a divorced woman, commits adultery.

On oaths

Mt5,33-37

tub Sma'ton ditamar lqadmaye:
Again you have heard that it has been said to those before:
dla tdaggel bmawmatak tSalle den Imarya mawmatak.
'Do not be false in your oath, fulfill your oath to the Lord.'
ana den amar-na Ikon la temrun sak: la baSmaiya
But I say to you: you should not swear at all, not by heaven,
dkurya-w dalaha
because it is the throne of God
wla bar'a dkubSa-w datxet riglawhi
nor by earth which is his footstool
apla boriSlem damditteh-y dmalka rabba
nor by Jerusalem, for it is a city of the great king
apla breSak te'ame dla miSkax att Ime'bbed
neither by your head you should swear for you cannot make
beh minta xada dsa'ara 'uqamta aw xiwwarta.
in it one part of the hair black or white.
ella tihwe millatkon: en en wla la:
But your words should be: 'Yes, Yes' and 'No, No:'
middem dmin halen yattir min biSa-w.
anything more than this is from evil.

24

On retaliation

Mt5,38-42

Sma'ton ditamar d'aina xalap 'aina wSinna xalap Sinna.
You have heard that it was said: 'Eye for eye and tooth for tooth.'
ana den amar-na Ikon: dla tqumun luqbal biSa ella
But I say to you: Do not stand against evil one, but
man dmaxe lak 'al pakkak dyammina apna leh ap xrena.
whoever strikes you on the right cheek, turn to him the other also.
wman dcabe daydun 'ammak wiSqol kottinak
And anyone who wants to sue you and take your shirt,
Sboq leh ap marTuTak.
let him have your coat also.
man damSaxxar lak mila xad zel 'ammeh trein.
Whoever forces you to go one mile, go with him two.
man dSa'el lak hab leh
He who asks you, give it to him,
wman dcabe dyezap minnak la tikleyuhi.
and who wants to borrow from you, do not refuse him.

On love of enemies

Mt5,43-48

Sma'ton ditamar: darxam lqarribak
You have heard that it was said: 'You shall love your neighbor
wasni lab'eldbabak.
and hate your enemy.'
ana den amar-na Ikon: axxebu lab'eldbabaikon wbarreku
But I say to you: Love your enemies and bless those,
Iman dla'eT Ikon wa'abedu dSappir Iman dsane Ikon
who curse you, and do good to those who hate you
wcallau 'al ailen ddabrin Ikon baqTira wradpin Ikon
and pray for those who take you by force and persecute you
aikanna dtihwon bnawhi dabukon dbaSmaiya
so that you may be the sons of your Father who is in heaven,
haw dmadnax SimSeh 'al Tabe w'al biSe
for he makes his sun rise upon the good and the evil
wmaxxet miTreh 'al zaddiqe w'al 'awwle.
and sends his rain upon the just and the unjust.
in ger maxbin-tton lailen dmaxbin Ikon mana agra it Ikon?
For if you love those who love you, what reward have you?
la ha ap makse hi hade 'abdin?
Do not even tax collectors do the same?
win Salin baSlama daxikon balxod mana yattir
And if you greet with peace only your brothers,
mana yattir 'abdin-tton: la ha ap makse hi hade 'abdin?
what more are you doing? Do not even tax collectors do the same?

25

hawau hakel atton gmire aikanna dabukon dbaSmaiya
Be, therefore, perfect even as your Father who is in heaven
gmir-u.
is perfect.

On almsgiving

Mt6,1-4

xuru den bzidqatkon dla te'bdunah qdam bnainaSa
Beware of your charity that you should not do it before men,
ak dtitixzon lhon win la agra lait lkon
so that you may be seen by them, otherwise you have no reward
lwat abukon dbaSmaiya.
from your Father who is in heaven.
emmati hakel d'abed att zediqta la tiqre qarna qdamaik
So when you give alms, do not sound a trumpet before you
ak d'abdin nasbai bappe baknuSata
as the hypocrites do in the synagogues
wabSuqe ak diStabbxun min bnainaSa.
and in the streets to be praised by men.
wamen amar-na lkon dqabbelu agrahon.
Truly I tell you, they have received their reward.
att den ma d'abed att zediqta la tida' semmalak
But when you give alms, do not let your left hand know
mana 'abda yamminak.
what the right hand is doing.
ak dtihwe zediqtak bkesya
so that your alms be in secret,
wabuk dxaze bkesya hu iper'ak bgilya.
and your Father who sees in secret will reward you openly.

On prayer

Mt6,5-6

wma damcalle att la tihwe ak nasbai bappe
And when you pray, do not be like hypocrites,
draxmin lamqam bknuSata wabzawyata dSuqe
for they love to stand in the synagogues and at the street corners
lamcallayu ditexzon labnainaSa.
to pray that they may be seen by the people.
wamen amar-na lkon dqabbelu agrahon.
And truly I tell you, they have received their reward.
att den emmati damcalle att 'ol ltawwanak waxxod tar'ak
But when you pray, go into your room and shut the door,
wcalla labuk dabkesya:
and pray to your Father in secret,

26

wabuk dxaze bkesya
and your Father who sees you in secret
iper'ak bgilya.
will reward you openly.
wma damcallein-tton
But when you pray,
la hawaiton mpaqqin ak xanpe
do not keep babbling as the Gentiles do,
sabrin ger dabmammla saggiya miStam'in.
for they hope that for their many words they will be heard.
la hakel tidmon lhon: abukon ger yada'
Therefore, do not be like them, for your Father knows
mana mitb'e lkon 'adla tiSalunaihi.
what you need before you ask him.

The Lord's Prayer - Matthew

Mt6,9-15

hakanna hakel callau atton:
This way, then, you should pray:

abun dbaSmaiya
Our Father who are in heaven,
itqaddaS Smak
hallowed be your name,
tete malkutak
your kingdom come,
ihwe cebyanak
your will be done
aikanna dbaSmaiya ap bar'a.
as it is in heaven so on earth.
hab lan laxma dsunqanan yawmana
Give us bread of our need today,
waSboq lan xawbain
and forgive us our debts
aikanna dap xnan Sbaqin lxaiyabain:
as we forgive our debtors,
wla ta"lan lnisyona
and lead us not into temptation
ella paccan min biSa.
but deliver us from evil.
miTTol ddilak malkuta wxaila wtiSbuxta
For yours is the kingdom and the power and the glory
l'alam 'almin.
for ever and ever.

27

The Lord's Prayer– Luke

L 11, 1-4

emmati damcallein-tton hakanna hawaiton amrin:
When you pray, say like this:
abun dbaSmaiya
Our Father who are in heaven,
itqaddaS Smak
hallowed be your name,
tete malkutak
your kingdom come,
ihwe cebyanak
your will be done
ak dbaSmaiya ap bar'a.
as it is in heaven so on earth.
hab lan laxma dsunqanan kollyom
Give us bread of our need every day,
waSboq lan xaTahain
and forgive us our sins,
ap xanan ger Sbaqin lkoll dxaiyabin lan:
for we ourselves forgive everyone who is indebted to us,
wla te"ellain lnisyona
and lead us not into temptation
ella proqain min biSa.
but deliver us from evil.

On forgiving

Mt6, 14-15 M11,25

wma dqaimin-tton lamcallayu Sboqu middem dit lkon
And whenever you stand praying, forgive if you have anything
'al naS dap abukon dbaSmaiya
against anyone, so that your Father who is in heaven
iSboq lkon sakelwatkon.
may also forgive your transgressions.
in den la tiSbequn labnainaSa
But if you do not forgive people,
apla abukon dbaSmaiya Sabeq lkon sakelwatkon.
neither your heavenly Father will forgive you your transgressions.

On fasting

Mt6, 16-18

emmati den dcaimin atton la tihwon kmire ak nasbai bappe:
And when you fast, do not look gloomy like the hypocrites do,
mxablin ger parcopaihon ak ditixzon labnainaSa dcaimin.
for they distort their faces that they may appear to men as fasting.

29

wamen amar-na lkon dqabbelu agrahon.
And truly I tell you that they have received their reward.
att den ma dca'em att aSSig appaik wamSox reSak
But when you fast, wash your face and anoint your head,
ak dla titxaze labnainaSa dca'em att
so that you should not be seen by men that you are fasting
ella labuk dabkesya
but by your Father in secret,
wabuk dxaze bkesya
and your Father who sees in secret
hu iper'ak.
he will reward you.

On treasures

Mt6,19-21

la tsimun lkon simata bar'a
Do not lay up for yourselves treasures on earth,
attar dsasa wakla mxablin
where moth and rust destroy,
waika dgannabe palSin wgannbin.
and where the thieves break in and steal.
ella simu lkon simata baSmaiya
But lay up for yourselves treasures in heaven,
aika dla sasa wakla mxablin
where neither moth nor rust destroy
waika dgannabe la palSin wla gannbin.
and where thieves do not break in and steal.
aika ger diteh simatkon tamman-u ap libbkon.
For where your treasure is, there is also your heart.

The straight eye

Mt6,22-23

Sraga dpagra iteh 'aina.
The lamp of the body is the eye.
in 'ainak hakel tihwe pSiTa
If then your eye is straight,
ap kulleh pagrak nahir-u.
your whole body will be full of light.
in den 'ainak tihwe biSa kulleh pagrak xeSSoka ihwe:
But if your eye is evil, your whole body will be darkness.
in hakel nuhara dbak xeSSoka-w:
If then the light in you is darkness,
xeSSokak kma ihwe!
your darkness how great it will be!

On serving two masters

Mt6,24 L 16,13

la naS miSkax latrein marawwan lmiplax
No one can serve two masters,
aw ger lxad isne wlaxrena irxam
for either he will hate one and love the other
aw ger lxad yaqqar wlaxrena iSuT.
or he will honor the one and neglect the other.
la meSikxin-tton lalaha lmiplax walmamona.
You cannot serve God and mammon.

On anxiety

Mt6,25-34

miTTol hana amar-na lkon: la tecpun lnapSkon
For this reason I tell you, do not be anxious about your life,
mana teklun wmana tiSton
what you will eat and what you will drink
wla lpagirkon wmana tilbeSun.
nor for your body, what you will wear.
la ha napSa yattira min saibarta wpagra min lbuSa?
Is life not more than food and the body than clothing?
xuru bparaxta daSmaiya dla zar'in wla xacdin wla xamlin
Look at the birds of the sky, they neither sow nor reap nor gather
bawcre wabukon dbaSmaiya mtarse lhon.
into barns and yet your Father who is in heaven feeds them.
la ha atton myattrin-tton minnhon?
Are you not worth much more than they?
mannu den minnkon kad yacep
And which of you by being anxious
miSkax lmawsapu 'al qawmteh amta xada?
can add to his stature one cubit?
w'al lbuSa mana yacpin-tton?
And about clothing why are you anxious?
itbaqqau bSoSanne ddabra aikanna rabyan
Consider the lilies of the wilderness, how they grow,
dla layan wla 'azlan.
they do not toil nor do they spin.
amar-na lkon den dapla Sleimon bkulleh Subxeh
Yet I tell you not even Solomon in all his glory
itkassi ak xada minnhen.
wa not clothed like one of these.
in den la'amira dxakla dyawmana itawhi
If then the grass of the field which is today
wamxar napel btanura
and tomorrow falls into the furnace,

31

alaha hakanna malbeS la saggi yattir Ikon z'orai haimanuta?
will God likewise not clothe you much more, you of little faith?
la hakel tecpun aw temrun: mana nekol?
Therefore, do not be anxious or say: What will we eat?
aw mana niSte aw mana nitkasse?
or what we will drink or what we will wear?
kollhen ger halen 'amme-w d'alma ba'ein lahen:
For all these things the Gentiles of the world seek,
abukon den dbaSmaiya yada'
for your Father who is in heaven knows
dap Ikon mitba'yan halen kullhen.
that you also need all those things.
ba'u den luqdam malkuteh dalaha wzaddiquteh
But seek first the kingdom of God and his righteousness
wkullhen halen mittawspan Ikon.
and all these things will be added to you.
la hakel tecpun damxar hu ger mxar yacep dileh.
So do not worry about tomorrow for tomorrow will care for itself
sapeq leh lyawma biSteh.
Sufficient for the day is its own evil.

On judging

Mt7,1-5 M4,24 L6,37

la tdunun dla titdinun.
Do not judge so that you will not be judged.
bdina ger ddainin-tton titdinun
For with the judgment that you judge, you will be judged
wbakyalta damkilin-tton mittekil Ikon.
and the measure you give will measure you get.
man dit leh ger itiheb leh
For to him who has will more be given
wman dlait leh ap haw dit leh iStqel minneh.
and from him who has not, even what he has will be taken away.
mana den xaze att gilla dab'aineh daxuk
Why do you see the straw that is in your brother's eye
wqarita dab'ainak la baxar att?
and the log which is in your own eye you do not notice?
aw aikanna amar att laxuk: Sboq appeq gilla
Or how can you say to your brother: 'Let me take the straw
min 'ainak wha qarita b'ainak?
out of your eye,' and look there is a log in your own eye?
naseb bappe appeq luqdam qarita min 'ainak
You hypocrite, first take the log out of your own eye,
whaiden itbxar lak Imappaqu gilla min 'aineh daxuk.
and the you see how to take straw out of your brother's eye.

32

Pearls before swine

Mt 7,6

la tittnun qudSa lkalbe
Do not give what is holy to dogs
wla tarmon marganyatkon qdam xazire
and do not throw your pearls before swine,
dalma iduSun innen briglaihon
or they will trample them under their feet,
wyehipkun ibaz'unakon.
then turn and mangle you.

The answer to prayers

Mt 7,7-11 L 11,9

Salu witiheb lkon b'au wtiSkxun
Ask and it will be given to you, seek and you will find,
qoSu witptax lkon.
knock and it will be opened to you.
koll ger dSa'el naseb wadba'e miSkax
For everyone who asks receives, and he who seeks finds,
wlaina dnaqeS mitiptax leh.
and to him who knocks it will be opened.
aw mannu minnkon gabra diSaliwhi breh laxma
Or what man of you, if his son asks him for bread,
lma kepa mawSeT leh?
will he hand him a stone?
win nuna iSaliwhi lma xiwya mawSeT leh?
and if he asks for a fish, will he hand him a serpent?
win hakel atton dbiSe atton
If you then, who are evil,
yad'in atton mawxbata Tabata lmintan labnaikon:
know how to give good gifts to your children,
kma yattira'it abukon dbaSmaiya
how much more will your Father who is in heaven
itten Tabata lailen dSalin leh.
give good things to those who ask him.
kma yattira'it abukon dbaSmaiya
How much more will your Father who is in heaven
itten ruxa qudSa lailen dSalin leh.
give Holy Spirit to those who ask him.

The golden rule

Mt 7,12

kollma dcabein-tton dye'bdun lkon bnainaSa
So whatever you wish that men would do to you,
hakanna ap atton 'abedu lhon: hanau ger oraita wanbiyye.
do so to them, for this is the law and the prophets.

The two gates

Mt7,13 L13,24

'olau btar'a 'allica dapte-w tar'a
Enter by the narrow gate, for the gate is wide,
warwixa urxa
and the road is broad
aida dmawbla labdana wsaggiye innon ailen dazin bah.
that leads to destruction and many enter through it.
ma qaTTin tar'a w'allica urxa
How small is the gate and narrow the road
aida dmawbla lxaiye waz'ore innon ailen dmiSkexin lah.
that leads to life and few are those who find it.
itkattaSu lme"al btar'a 'allica:
Strive to enter through the narrow gate,
amar-na lkon ger dsaggiye ib'on lme"al wla iSkxun.
I tell you, many will seek to enter and will not be able.

False prophets

Mt7,15-17 L6,43

izdahru min nbiyye daggale
Beware of false prophets,
datein lwatkon balbuSe dimre
who come to you in sheep's clothing
min lgaww den itaihon debe xaTope.
but inwardly are ravenous wolves.
min peraihon den tid'un innon.
But you will know them by their fruits.
lma laqTin min kubbe 'inbe aw min qurTbe tene?
Do they gather grapes from thorns or figs from thistles?

Good and bad fruits

Mt7,17-20

hakanna koll ilana Taba pere Sappire 'abed
Even so every good tree bears good fruits,
ilana den biSa pere biSe 'abed.
but the bad tree bears bad fruits.
la miSkax ilana Taba pere biSe lme'bbad
A good tree cannot bear bad fruits
wla ilana biSa pere Tabe lme'bbad
nor can a bad tree bear good fruits.
kol ilana dla 'abed pere Tabe mitpseq
Every tree that does not bear good fruits is cut
wabnura napel.
and thrown into the fire.
maden min peraihon tid'un innon.
Thus by their fruits you will know them.

The true disciple

Mt7,21-23

la wa koll damar li: mari mari
Not everyone who says to me: 'My Lord, my Lord,'
'a'el Imalkuta daSmaiya
will enter the kingdom of heaven
ella man d'abed cibyaneh dabi dbaSmaiya.
but he who does the will of my Father who is in heaven.
saggiye yemrun li bhaw yawma: mari mari
Many will say to me on that day: 'My Lord, my Lord,
la baSmak itnabbin
did we not in your name prophesy
wbaSmak Sede appeqn
and in your name cast out demons
wbaSmak xaile saggiye 'abadn?
and in your name perform many miracles?'
whaiden awdde Ihon: dmimmtom la ida'tkon
And then I will declare to them: 'I never knew you,
arxequ Ikon menni palxai 'awla!
go away from me, you evildoers!'

The two foundations

Mt7,24-27 L6,47-49

koll hakel dSama' millai halen w'abed lahen
Everyone then who hears these words of mine and does them
itdamme Igabra xakkima haw dabna baiteh 'al So'a
will be like a wise man who built his house upon the rock
wanxet miTra wettau naharawata wanSabu ruxe
and the rain fell and the floods came and the winds blew
witTariyu beh bbaita haw wla napal
and beat upon the house, but it did not fall,
Satasahwi ger 'al So'a siman wai:
because its foundation was laid upon the rock.
wkoll man dSama' millai halen
Everyone who hears these words of mine
wla 'abed lahen:
and does not do them,
itdamme Igabra sakla dabna baiteh 'al xala:
will be like foolish man who built his house on the sand
wanxet miTra wettau naharawata wanSabu ruxe
and the rain fell and the floods came and the winds blew
witTariyu bbaita haw
and beat against the house,
wanpal wahawat mapulteh rabba:
and it fell and its fall was great.

35

THE SERMON ON THE PLAIN   *According to Luke*

THE BEATITUDES
                                    L 6,20-23

Tubaikon miskene
Blessed are you who are poor,
ddilkon-y malkuta dalaha.
for yours is the kingdom of God.
Tubaikon ailen dkapnin haSa
Blessed are you who are hungry now,
dtisibb'un.
for you will be satisfied.
Tubaikon ladbakein haSa dtigixkun.
Blessed are you who weep now, for you will laugh.
Tubaikon ma dsanin Ikon bnainaSa
Blessed are you when men hate you
wamparSin Ikon wamxassedin Ikon
and when they exclude you and insult you
wmapqin Simkon ak biSe
and denounce your name as evil,
xalap breh dnaSa.
because of the Son of man.
xadau bhaw yawma wducu
Rejoice on that day and leap for joy,
dagrikon saggi baSmaiya.
because your reward is great in heaven.
hakanna ger 'abdin wau abahaton lanbiyye.
for so their fathers did to the prophets.

THE WOES
                                    L 6,24-26

bram wai Ikon 'attire
But woe to you who are rich,
dqabbelton buyakon.
for you have received your consolation.
wai Ikon sab'e dtikpnun.
woe to you who are full, for you will be hungry.
wai Ikon ladgaxkin haSa dtibhon wtitablun.
Woe to you who laugh now, for you will mourn and weep.
wai Ikon kad ihwon amrin 'alaikon bnainaSa dSappir
Woe to you when all men speak well of you,
hakanna ger 'abdin wau lanbiyye ddaggaluta abahaton.
for so their fathers did to the false prophets.

37

On love of one's enemies

Ikon den amar-na ladSam'in: axxebu lab'eldbabakon
But I tell you that hear: Love your enemies,
wa'abedu dSappir lailen dsanein Ikon
do good to those who hate you,
wbarreku lailen dlaiTin Ikon
bless those who curse you,
wcallau 'al ailen ddabrin Ikon baqTira.
and pray for those who take you with violence.
wladmaxe lak 'al pakkak qarreb leh xrena:
To him who strikes you on your cheek, offer to him the other;
wmin man dSaqel marTuTak la tikle ap kottinak.
and from him who takes your coat, do not withhold even your shirt.
Ikoll dSa'el lak hab leh
To everyone who asks you give to him,
wmin man dSaqel dilak la titba'.
and from him who takes your goods do not demand it back.
waikanna dcabein-tton di'bbedun Ikon bnainaSa
And as you wish that men would do to you,
hakwat 'abedu lhon ap atton.
likewise do to them you also.
in ger maxxabin-tton lailen dmaxxabin Ikon
If you love those who love you,
aida-y Taibutkon?
what is your credit?
ap ger xaTTaye lailen dmaxxabin lhon raxmin.
For even sinners love those who love them.
win 'abdin-tton dTab lailen dmaTibin Ikon
And if you do good to those who do good to you
aida-y Taybutkon?
what is your credit?
ap xaTTaye ger hakanna 'abdin.
For even the sinners likewise do.
win mawzpin-tton lman dsabrin-tton dtitpar'un minneh
and if you lend to one when you expect to be repaid by him,
aida-y Taibutkon?
what is your credit?
ap xaTTaye ger lxaTTaye ger mawzpin dhakanna itpar'un.
Even sinners lend to sinners that they might be repaid.
bram axxebu lab'eldbabaikon waTebu Ikon
But love your enemies and do good to them
wawzepu wla tipisqun sabra dnaS
and lend and do not cut off the hope of anyone,

wihwe saggi agirkon
and your reward will be great,
wtihwon bnawhi drama
and you will be the sons of the Most High,
dhu bassim-u 'al biSe w'al kapore.
for he is kind to the evil and the ungrateful.
hawau hakel raxmane aikanna dap abukon mraxmana-u.
Be, therefore, merciful even as your Father is merciful.

On judging

L6,37-42

la tdunun wla mittdinin-tton:
Do not judge and you will not be judged;
la txaiybun wla mitxaiyebin-tton.
do not condemn and you will not be condemned.
Srau wtiStron : habu wmitiheb lkon
forgive and you will be forgiven; give and it will be given to you.
bakyalta Tabta warqi'ta wamSappa'ta
in good measure and pressed down and abundant
yarmon b'ubbaikon.
will be poured into your lap.
bhai ger kyalta damkilin-tton mittkil lkon.
For the measure with which you measure it will be measured to you.
Ima miSkax samya Isamya lamdabbaru?
Can a blind man lead a blind man?
la traihon bgummaca naplin?
Will they not both fall into a pit?
lait talmida dyattir min rabbeh
A disciple is not greater than his teacher,
koll naS ger dagmir ihwe ak rabbeh.
for everyone who is perfect should be like his teacher.
mana den xaze att gilla dab'aineh daxuk
Why do you see the speck that is in your brother's eye,
qarita den dab'ainak la mitxazya lak?
but do not notice the log that is in your own eye?
aw aikanna miSkax att lmemar laxuk:
Or how can you say to your brother:
axi Sboq appeq gilla min 'ainak
Brother, let me take out the speck from your eye,
dha qarita dab'ainak dilak la mitxazya lak?
when you yourself do not see the log that is in your own eye?
naseb bappe appeq luqdam qarita min 'ainak whaiden
You hypocrite, first take out the log from your own eye, and then
itixze lak lmappaqu gilla min 'aineh daxuk.
you will see clearly to take out the speck from your brother's eye.

By their fruits...

L6,43-45

la it ilana Taba d'abed pere biSe
No good tree bears bad fruits,
apla ilana biSa d'abed pere Tabe
nor does a bad tree bear good fruits:
kol ilana ger min perawhi-w mitida'
for every tree by its fruits is known.
la ger laqTin min kubbe tene
For they do not gather figs from thorns,
apla min sanya qaTpin 'inbe
nor they gather grapes from a bramble bush.
gabra Taba min simata Tabata dablibbeh
The good man out of the good treasure of his heart
mappeq Tabata
produces good,
wgabra biSa min simata biSata dablibbeh
and the evil man out of his evil treasure of his heart
mappeq biSata.
produces evil.
min tawtaray libba ger mmallan sipwata.
for from the abundance of the heart the lips speak.

The house built upon the rock

L6,46-49

mana qarein-tton li: mari mari
Why do you call me: 'My Lord, my Lord,'
wmiddem damar-na la 'abdin-tton?
and what I tell you are not doing?
koll naS date lwati wSama' millai w'abed lahen
Every one who comes to me and hears my words and does them,
exawweikon lmana dame:
I will show you what he is like:
dame lgabra dabna baita wxapar w'ammeq
he is like a man who built a house and dug deep,
wsam Satesta 'al So'a
and laid the foundation upon rock:
kad hawa den mil'a ittTari mil'a bbaita haw
and when the flood arose and the flood beat against that house,
wla iSkax danzi'iwhi sima wat ger Satesteh 'al So'a.
and could not shake it, for its foundation was placed on rock.
whaw Sama' wla 'abed dame lgabra
But he who hears and does not do, is like a man
dabna baiteh 'al 'apra dla Satesta
who built a house on soil without the foundation;

40

wkad ittTari beh nahara bar Sa'teh npal
and when the stream beat against it, immediately it fell,
whawat mapulteh rabba dbaita haw.
and great was the fall of that house.

The centurion of Capernaum

Mt8,7-13 L7,1-10

ana ate wasseyuhi.
I will come and heal him.
amen amar-na lkon dapla bisrayel eSkxet ak hade haimanuta.
Truly I tell you, not even in Israel have I found such faith.
amar-na lkon den dsaggiye yeton min madinxa
I tell you, many will come from the east
wmin ma'arba wistamkun 'am abraham wisxaq wya'qob
and the west and will recline with Abraham, Isaac and Jacob
bmalkuta daSmaiya
in the kingdom of heaven,
bneh den dmalkuta ippqun lxeSSoka barraya.
but the sons of the kingdom will be thrown into the outer darkness.
tamman ihwe bikya wxuraq Sinne.
There will be weeping and gnashing of teeth.
zel aikanna dhaiment ihwe lak.
Go, as you have believed, let it be done for you.

The widow's son at Nain

L7,13-14

la tibkein!
Do not weep!
'alaima lak amar-na qum!
Young man, I say to you, rise!

On following Jesus - to a scribe

L9,60 Mt8,20

Ita'le niq'e it lhon walparaxta daSmaiya maTlela
Foxes have holes and birds of the sky have nests,
labreh den dnaSa lait leh aika dismok reSeh.
but the Son of man has nowhere to lay his head.
ta batari waSboq lmite qabrin mitaihon
Come after me and leave the dead to bury their own dead;
watt zel sabbar malkuteh dalaha
but as for you, go and preach the kingdom of God.
la naS rame ideh 'al xarba dpaddana wxa'ar lbestreh
No one who puts his hand on the plow and looks back,
wxaSax lmalkuteh dalaha.
is fit for the kingdom of God.

41

Stilling the storm

M4,39 Mt8,26

Sli! zgir att!
Quiet! Be still!
lmana daxultanin-tton hakanna? wlmana lait bkon haimanuta?
Why are you so afraid? And why there is no faith in you?

The Gerasene demons

M5,8-19 L8,35 Mt8,28

poq min barnaSa ruxa Tanpa: aikanna Smak?
Come out of man, you unclean spirit! What is your name?
zel lbaitak lwat naSaik wiSta'a lhon
Go to your home to your friends and tell them
middem da'abad lak marya uditraxam 'alaik.
what the Lord has done for you and how he had mercy on you.

A woman with a hemorrhage

L8,45-48 M5,25-34 Mt9,20-22

mannu qreb lmanai?
Who touched my clothes?
naS qreb li: ana ger yed'et dxaila npaq menni:
Someone touched me; for I know that power has gone out from me.
itlabbabi brati haimanuteki axyateki.
Take heart, my daughter, your faith has made you well.
zeli baSlama wahwaiti xalima min maxoteki!
Go in peace, and be healed of your disease!

Jairus' daughter

M5,36 Mt9,24 L8,49

la tirxal balxod haimen!
Do not fear, only believe!
mana rxibin-tton wbakein?
Why make a commotion and weep?
proqu lkon Talita ger la mitat ella damka-y.
Depart you all, for the girl is not dead, but is sleeping.
Talita qumi!
Little girl, arise!

Two blind men

Mt9,28 M10,51

mana cabe att e'bbed lak?
What do you want me to do for you?
mhaimin atton dmiSkax-na hade lme'bbad?
Do you believe that I am able to do this?

aikanna dhaimenton ihwe Ikon.
As you have believed it let it be to you.
xazaw Ima naS ida'.
See that no one knows it.

The harvest is great

Mt9,37-38

xacada saggi wpa'le z'orin.
The harvest is great, but workers are few.
b'au hakel min mare xacada dyappeq pa'le Ixacada.
Pray then the Lord of harvest to send workers to his harvest.

Sending out disciples

Mt10,5-16

burxa dxannpe la tezun
In the way of Gentiles do not go
wlamditta dSamraye la te"lun
and the cities of the Samaritans do not enter
zelu Ikon den yattira'it Iwat 'irbe debbadu min beit israyel
but go rather to the lost sheep of the house of Israel
wkad azin-tton akrezu wemaru:
and as you go, preach saying:
dqirbat malkuta daSmaiya.
The kingdom of heaven is at hand.
krihe assau wgarbe dakkau wdaiwe appequ
Heal the sick, cleanse lepers, cast out demons.
maggan nsabton maggan habu.
Freely you received, freely give.
la tiqnon dahaba wla sema wla nxaSa bkisaikon
Do not take gold nor silver nor copper in your money belts,
wla tarmala lurxa wla tartein kottinyan wla msane
nor bag for your journey nor two coats nor shoes
wla SabTa: Sawe-w ger pa'la saibarteh.
nor staff: for the worker deserves his food.
laida den mditta aw qrita d'allin-tton lah
And whatever city or village you enter,
Sa'elu mannu Sawe bah
inquire who is worthy in it,
wtamman hawau 'adamma dnapqin-tton.
and stay there until you depart,
wma d'allin-tton Ibaita Salu Slameh dbaita
And as you enter the house, greet with peace the family
winhu Sawe baita Slamkon yete 'alawhi
and if the house is worthy, your peace will come upon it,
in den la Sawe Slamkon 'alaikon ipne.
but if it is not worthy, your peace will return to you.

44

man dla den mqabbel lkon wla Sma' millaikon
Whoever does not receive you or listen to your words,
kad napqin-tton min baita aw min qrita hai:
as you go out of that house or village,
pecu hilla min riglaikon.
shake the dust off your feet.
wamen amar-na lkon dlar'a dasdom wad'amora
Truly I tell you, for the land of Sodom and Gomorrah
ihwe nix byawma ddina aw lamditta hai.
it will be easier in the of judgment than for that city.

The fate of the disciples
Mt10,16-25
ha ana mSaddar-na lkon ak imre bainai debe
See, I am sending you out like sheep among wolves,
hawau hakel xakkime ak xawawata wtammime ak yawne.
so be wise as serpents and innocent as doves.
izdaru den min bnainaSa: maSilmin lkon ger lbeit daiyane
Beware of men, for they will hand you over to the courts
wbaknuSathon inagdunakon waqdam hegmone wmalke
and in their synagogues flog you and before governors and kings
mqarbin lkon miTTolati lsahaduta dilhon wad'amme.
you will be dragged for my sake as a witness before them and
the Gentiles.
emmati den dyaSilmunakon
But when they hand you over,
la tecpun aikanna aw mana tmallun:
do not worry about how or what you are to say,
mitiheb lkon ger bhai Sa'ta ma datmallun:
for it will be given to you in that hour what you are to say;
la wa ger atton mmallin
for it is not you who speak
ella ruxa dabukon mmalla bkon.
but the Spirit of your Father speaking in you.

Coming persecutions
Mt10,21-25
yaSlem den axxa laxxuh lmawta waba labreh
Brother will betray his brother to death and the father his son
waiqumun bnaiya 'al abahahon waimitun innon.
and the children will rise up against their parents and slay them.
wtihwon sni'in min kollnaS miTTol Semi
And you will be hated by all men because of my name,
aina den daisabbar 'adamma lxarta hu ixxe.
but he who endures to the end will be saved.

45

ma dradpin lkon den bamditta hade 'aroqu lkon laxreta
When they persecute you in one town, flee to the next,
amen ger amar-na lkon dla tSalmun innen kullhen mdinata
for truly I say to you, you will not finish all the towns
dbeit israyel 'adamma dyete breh dnaSa.
of the house of Israel before the Son of man comes.
lait talmida dyattir min rabbeh wla 'abda min mareh:
A disciple is not above his teacher nor a servant above his master,
sapeq leh ltalmida dihwe ak rabbeh
it is enough for the disciple to be like his teacher
wal'abda ak mareh.
and for the servant like his master.
in lmareh dbaita qrau b'elzebub
If they have called the master of the house Beelzebub
xad kma lbnai baiteh.
how much more those of his household.

Fearless confession

Mt10,26-33 L12,2-9
la hakel tidexlun minnhon lait ger middem dakse
Therefore, do not fear them, for there is nothing concealed
dla itgle wdamTaSSai dla itida':
that will not be revealed or hidden that will not be known.
middem damar-na likon bxeSSoka umruhi atton bnahira
What I tell you in darkness, speak in the light
wmiddem dbidnaikon Sam'in-tton akrezu 'al iggare.
and what you hear in your ears, proclaim upon the housetops.
wla tidexlun min ailen dqaTlin pagra
And do not fear those who kill the body
napSa den la miSkxin lmiqTal
but cannot kill the soul,
dxalu den yattira'it min man dmiSkax
rather fear him who can
dalnapSa walpagra yawbed bgehanna:
both soul and body destroy in hell.
la tartein ciprin mizdabbnan bassar?
Are not two sparrows sold for a penny?
wxada minnhen bil'ad min abukon la napla 'al ar'a.
And not one of them without your Father falls to the ground.
dilkon den ap minne dreSkon kullhen manyan innen.
But as for you, even the hairs of your head are all numbered,
la hakel tidexlun min cipre saggiyata myattrin-tton.
So do not fear, than many sparrows you are more valuable.
koll naS hakel dyawde bi qdam bnainaSa
Therefore, everyone who confesses me before men,

awdde beh ap ana qdam abi dbaSmaiya.
I will also confess him before my Father who is in heaven.
man den dikpor bi qdam bnainaSa
But whoever denies me before men,
ekpor beh ap ana qdam abi dbaSmaiya.
I will also deny him before my Father who is in heaven.

Divisions within households

Mt10,34-36 L12,51

la tisbrun detteit darme Saina bar'a
Do not think that I came to bring peace on the earth,
la etteit darme Saina ella xarba.
I did not come to bring peace, but a sword.
etteit ger deplog gabra 'al abuhi
For I have come to set a man against his father,
wbarta 'al immah
and a daughter against her mother
wkallta 'al xamatah
and a daughter-in-law against her mother-in-law
wab'eldbabawhi dgabra bnai baita.
and enemies of a man are those of his household.
man draxem aba aw imma yattir min dli la Sawe li:
He who loves father or mother more than me is not worthy of me,
wman draxem bra aw barta yattir min dli la Sawe li:
and he who loves son or daughter more than me is not worthy of me.
wkoll dla Saqel zqipeh wate batari la Sawe li.
He who does not take his cross and follow me is not worthy of me.
man diSkax napSeh yawbdih
He who finds his life will lose it
wman dyawbed napSeh miTTolati iSkxih.
and he who loses his life for my sake will find it.

Rewards

Mt10,40-42

man damqabbel lkon li mqabbel
He who receives you receives me,
wman dli qabbel lman dSalxani mqabbel.
and he who receives me receives him who sent me.
man damqabbel nbyya bSem nbiyya
He who receives a prophet in the name of a prophet
agra danbiyya naseb
will receive a prophet's reward
wman damqabbel zaddiqa bSem zaddiqa
and he who receives a just man in the name of a just man

agra dzaddiqa naseb.
will receive a just man's reward.
wkoll dmaSqe lxad min halen z'ore
And whoever gives to drink to one of these little ones
kasa dqarrire balxod baSma dtalmida
even a cup of cold water in the name of a disciple,
amen amar-na lkon dla yawbed agreh.
truly I tell you, he will not lose his reward.

John the Baptist

Mt11,4-15
zel iSta"au lyoxannan ailen dSam'in atton wxazein:
Go and tell John those things which you hear and see:
smaiya xazein waxagire mhallkin wgarbe mitdakkein
the blind see and the lame walk and the lepers are cleansed
wxarSe Sam'in wmite qaimin
and the deaf hear and the dead are raised up
wmiskene mistabbrin
and the poor are given hope,
wTubawhi laina dla itkSel bi.
and blessed is he who is not offended in me.
mana npaqton lxurba lmexza?
What did you go out into wilderness to see?
qanya dmin ruxa mittezi'?
A reed shaken by the wind?
win la mana npaqton lmexza?
And if not, what did you go out to see?
gabra dnaxta rakkike lbiS?
A man wearing soft clothes?
ha ailen drakkike lbiSin beit malke innon.
Behold, those who wear soft clothes are in kings' houses.
win la mana npaqton lmexza nbiyya?
And if not, what did you go out to see? A prophet?
en amarna-na lkon wyattir min nbiyya.
Yes, I tell you, and more than a prophet.
hanaw ger da'alawhi ktibi:
For this is he about whom it is written:
dha ana mSaddar-na malaki qdam parcopak
'Behold, I send my messenger before your face
dyatqqen urxa qdamaik.
to prepare the way before you.'
amen amar-na lkon dla qam bilidai niSSe
Truly, I tell you that no one stands among those born of women
drab min yoxannan ma'amdana:
greater than John the Baptist,

48

z'ora den bmalkut Smaiya rabb-u minneh.
yet who is least in the kingdom of heaven is greater than he.
min yawmai yoxannan den ma'amdana wa'adamma IhaSa
For from the days of John the Baptist until now
malkuta daSmaiya baqTira midabra
the kingdom of heaven suffers violence
waqTirane mxaTTpin lah.
and the violent ones are robbing it.
kullhon ger nbiyye woraita 'adamma lyoxannan itnabbiyu.
For all the prophets and the Law until John prophesied.
win cabein atton qabbelu dhuyu eliyya da'atid Imeta.
And if you are willing to accept it, he is Elias who is to come.
man dit leh idne diSma' iSma'.
He who has ears to hear, let him hear.

This generation
Mt11,16-19

Iman den edammeih ISarbta hade?
But to what shall I compare this generation?
damya laTlaye dyatbin bSuqa wqa'ein Ixabraihon
It is like children sitting in the market and calling to their friends
wamrin: zmarin Ikon wla raqqidton
and saying: 'We played the flute for you and you did not dance,
wallain Ikon wla arqedton.
we wailed for you and you did not mourn.'
etta ger yoxannan dla akel wla Sate
For John came neither eating nor drinking,
wamrin: daiwa it beh.
and they say: 'He has a demon.'
etta breh dnaSa akel wSate wamrin:
The Son of man came eating and drinking, and they say:
ha gabra akola wSate xamra wraxma dmakse
'See, a glutton, a wine drinker and a friend of tax collectors
wadxaTTaye: wizddadqat xekkimta min 'abadeh.
and sinners!' Yet wisdom is justified by her deeds.

Woes to the cities
Mt11,20 L10,12

wai leki kurzin: wai leki beit caiyada!
Woe to you Chorazin! Woe to you Bethsaida!
dillu bcor wabcaidon hawau xaile ailen dahawau bken
For if in Tyre and Sidon had been those miracles that were in you,
kbar den bsaqqe wabqiTma tabu.
doubtless, in sackcloth and ashes they would have repented.

49

bram amar-na Iken dalcor walcaidan ihwe nix
But I tell you, for Tyre and Sidon will be easier
byawma ddina aw Iken.
in the day of judgment than for you.
watt kpar naxom hai da'adamma laSmaiya ittrimti
And you, Capernaum, which have been exalted to heaven
'adamma laSyol tittaxtten.
to Sheol you will be brought down.
dillu basdom hawau xaile ailen dahawau beki
For if in Sodom had been those miracles that were in you,
qaiyama wat 'adamma lyawmana.
she would be standing to this day.
bram amar-na leki dlar'a dasdom ihwe nix
But I tell you that for the land of Sodom will be easier
byawma ddina aw leki.
on the day of judgment than for you.

The praise of the Father

Mt11,25-27 L10,21-22

mawdde-na lak abi mara daSmaiya wdar'a
I give praise to you, my Father, Lord of heaven and earth,
dkassitt halen min xakkime wsakkultane
that you have hidden these things from the wise and learned
waglait innen lyallude.
and have revealed them to infants.
en abi dhakanna hawa cibyana qdamaik.
Yes, Father, for such was your pleasure before you.
koll middem iStlem li min abi
All things have been delivered to me by my Father,
wla naS yada' labra ella in aba
and no one knows the Son except the Father
apla laba naS yada' ella in bra
nor does anyone know the Father except the Son
walman dcabe bra digle.
and anyone to whom the Son chooses to reveal.

His yoke

Mt11,28-30

tau lwati kullhon laiya waSqilai mawble
Come to me all who labor and carry burdens
wana annixakon.
and I will give you rest.
Sqolu niri 'alaikon willapu menni dnix-na
Bear my yoke upon you and learn from me, for I am gentle

wmakkik-na blebbi wmiSkxin-tton nyaxa InapSatkon.
and humble in heart, and you will find rest for your souls.
niri ger bassim-u wmawbali qallila-y.
For my yoke is pleasant and my burden is light.

The woman with the ointment

L7,40-50

Sim'on middem it li demar lak:
Simon, I have something to say to you.
trein xaiyabe it waw lxad mare xawba:
There were two debtors to a creditor:
xad xaiyab wa deinare xammeSma waxrena deinare xamSin.
one owed five hundred denarii and the other fifty denarii.
wadlait wa lhon lmipra' latraihon Sbaq.
And because they had no way to repay, he forgave them both.
aina hakel minnhon yattir yaxbiwhi?
Now which of them will love him more?
trica'it dant: xaze att attta hade?
You have judged rightly. Do you see this woman?
Ibaitak 'ellet: maiya lriglai la yabt:
I entered your house; you gave me no water for my feet,
hade den bdim'eh riglai cabb'at
but she with her tears has wet my feet
wabsa'arah Sawyat innon:
and with her hair dried them.
att la nSaqtani hade den ha min d'ellat
You gave me no kiss; but she, since I came in,
la Silit riglai lamnaSSaqu.
has not ceased to kiss my feet.
att miSxa lreSi la mSaxet:
You did not anoint my head with oil,
hade den bmiSxa dbisma riglai miSxat.
but she anointed my feet with perfume.
xalap hade amar-na lak
For this reason I say to you,
daSbiqin lah xaTaheh saggiye
her sins are forgiven, which are many,
miTTol dahabat saggi.
because she loved much.
haw den dqallil miStbeq leh qallil maxxeb.
But he who is forgiven little, loves little.
Sbiqin leki xaTahaiki.
Your sins have been forgiven you.
haimanuteki axyateki: zeli baSlama!
Your faith has saved you. Go in peace!

51

Jesus and Beelzebub

Mt12,25-30

koll malku dtitpallag 'al napSah texrab
Every kingdom divided against itself will be destroyed,

wkoll bai wamdina ditpallag 'al napSeh la iqum.
and any house or city divided against itself will not stand.

win saTana IsaTana mappeq 'al napSeh itpallag
And if Satan casts out Satan, he is divided against himself,

aikanna hakel qaima malkuteh?
how then will his kingdom stand?

win ana bab'elzebub mappeq-na daiwe
And if I cast out demons by Beelzebub,

bnaikon bmana mapqin lhon?
by whom do your sons cast them out?

miTTol hana hinnon ihwon lkon daiyane.
Therefore, they shall be judges of you.

win bruxa dalaha ana mappeq-na daiwe
But if it is by the Spirit of God that I cast out demons,

qerbat lah aikanna malkuta dalaha.
then it has come near to you the kingdom of God.

aw aikanna naS miSkax dye"ol lbeit lxassina
Or how can one enter a strong man's house

wmanawhi ibboz ella in luqdam yesriwhi lxassina?
and plunder his goods, unless he first binds the strong man?

whaiden baiteh ibboz.
Then he may plunder his house.

man dla wa 'ammi luqbali-u:
He who is not with me is against me,

wman dla kanneS 'ammi mbaddaru mbaddar.
and he who does not gather with me scatters.

The sin against the Holy Spirit

Mt12,31-37

miTTol hana amar-na lkon dkoll xaTahin
Therefore, I tell you that all sins

wguddapin iStabqun labnainaSa:
and blasphemies will be forgiven men,

guddapa den d'al ruxa la iSitbeq labnainaSa:
but blasphemy against the Spirit will not be forgiven men.

wkoll ma dyemar millta 'al breh dnaSa iStbeq leh:
And whoever says a word against the Son of man will be forgiven.

koll den d'al ruxa dqudSa yemar
But anyone who will speak against the Holy Spirit,

la iSitbeq leh la b'alma hana wla b'alma da'atid.
will not be forgiven either in this world or in the world to come.

A tree and its fruits

Mt12,33-37

aw 'abedu ilana Sappira wperawhi Sappire
Either make the tree good and its fruits good,
aw 'abedu ilana biSa wperawhi biSe
or make the tree bad and its fruits bad,
min perawhi-w ger mitida' ilana.
for by its fruit the tree is known.
yalda dakedne: aikanna miSkxin-tton Tabata lammallalu
You brood of vipers! How can you speak good things
dbiSe atton?
when you are evil?
min tawtarai libba ger mmallel puma.
For out of abundance of the heart speaks the mouth.
gabra Taba min simata Tabata mappeq Tabata
The good man out of his good treasure brings forth good,
wgabra biSa min simata biSata mappeq biSata.
and evil man out of his evil treasure brings forth evil.
amar-na Ikon ger dkoll milla baTTala dyemrun bnainaSa
But I tell you, for every careless word the people speak,
itnun pitgamai byawma ddina.
they will give an accounting in the day of judgment.
min millaik ger tizddadaq
For by your words you will be justified,
wmin millaik titxaiyab.
and by your words you will be condemned.

The sign of Jonah

Mt12,39 M8,12 L11,29

Sarbta biSta wgaiyarta ata ba'ya
A generation, evil and adulterous, seeks for a sign,
wata la titiheb lah ella ateh dyawnan nbiyya.
but no sign will be given except the sign of Jonah the prophet.
aikanna ger dahawa yawnan bkarseh dnuna
For as Jonah was in the belly of the fish
tlata imamin wtlata lailawan hakanna ihwe breh dnaSa
for three days and three nights, so will be the Son of man
blibbah dar'a tlata imamin wtlata lailawan.
in the heart of the earth three days and three nights.
gabre ninwaye iqumun bdina 'am Sarbta hade
The men of Ninive will rise in judgment with this generation
waixayibunah dhinnon tabu bkarozuteh dyawnan
and condemn it, for they repented at the preaching of Jonah,
wha drab min yawnan tnan.
and behold, something is greater than Jonah is here.

malkta dtaimna tqum
The queen of the south will rise
bdina 'am Sarbta hade watxayibih
in judgment with this generation and condemn it,
dettat min 'ibreh dar'a
for she came from the ends of the earth
dtiSma' xekkimteh daSleimon
to hear the wisdom of Solomon,
wha dyattir min Sleimon harka.
and behold, someone is greater than Solomon is here.

The return of the evil spirit

Mt12,43 L11,24

emmati den druxa Tanpta tippoq min barnaSa
Now when the unclean spirit goes out of the man,
mitkarka batrawata dmaiya lait bhon wba'ya nyaxa
it roams through waterless places seeking rest,
wla miSkxa.
and does not find it.
haiden amra:
Then it says:
ehppoq lbaiti min aika dnipqet.
'I will return to my house from which I came.'
watya miSkxa dasriq waxamim wamcabbat.
And when it comes, it finds empty, swept and furnished.
haiden aza dabra 'ammah Sba' ruxe xranyan
Then it goes and takes along with it seven other spirits
dminnah biSan w'allan w'amran beh
more evil than itself and they enter and live there,
whawya xarteh dgabra haw biSa min qadmaiteh.
and the end of that man becomes worse than the first.
hakanna ihwe lah lSarbta hade biSta.
So will it be also with this evil generation.

The true family

Mt12,48 L8.21

man-i emmi wman innon axai?
Who is my mother and who are my brothers?
ha emmi wha axai!
Here are my mother and my brothers!
koll naS den d'abed cibyaneh dabi dbaSmaiya
For whoever does the will of my Father in heaven
huyu axi wxati wemmi.
is my brother and my sister and my mother.

The parable of the sower

Mt13,3-9 M4,3-9 L8,5-8

ha npaq zaro'a Imizra'
Behold, the sower went out to sow
wkad zra' it danpal 'al yad urxa
and as he sowed, some of it fell beside the road,
wettat paraxta wekalteh.
and the birds came and ate them up.
waxrena npal 'al So'a aika dlait wa medra saggiya
Others fell on the rocks where was not much soil
wbar Sa'teh Swax miTTol dlait wa 'umqa dar'a.
and at once they sprouted, since they had no depth of soil.
kad dnax den SimSa xam:
But when sun came up, they were scorched,
wmiTTol dlait wa leh 'iqqara ibeS.
and because they had no root they dried up.
waxrena npal beit kubbe
Others fell among the thorns,
waslequ kubbe wxankuhi.
and the thorns came up and choked them out.
waxrena npal bar'a Tabta wyab pere
And others fell on the good soil and produced fruit,
it dma' wit deStin wit datlatin.
some a hundredfold, some sixty, and some thirty.
man dit leh idne diSma' iSma'!
Who has ears to hear, let him hear!

The purpose of parables

Mt13,11-17

dalkon-u ihib Imidda' raza dmalkuta daSmaiya
To you it is given to know the mystery of the kingdom of heaven,
lhannon den la ihib.
but to them it is not given.
Iman ger dit leh itiheb leh wityattar leh
For to him who has will be given and it shall increase to him
walman dlait leh wap haw dit leh iSitqel minneh.
and who has not, even what he has will be taken from him.
miTTol hana bpellata mmallel-na 'ammhon
Therefore in parables I speak to them,
miTTol dxazein wla xazein wSam'in wla Sam'in
because seeing they do not see, and hearing they do not hear
wla mistakklin.
nor do they understand.
waSlama bhon nbyuteh deSa'ya demar:
With the it is fulfilled the prophecy of Isaiah which says:

dSima'a tiSim'un wla tistakklun
'Hearing you will hear but will not understand
wmexza texzon wla tid'un.
and seeing you will see but will not perceive.
it'abbi leh ger libbeh d'amma hana
For the heart of this people has become dull
ubidnaihon yaqqira'it Sma'u
and with their ears they are hard of hearing
w'ainaihon 'ammecu
and their eyes they have closed,
dla yexzon b'ainaihon wiSm'un bidnaihon
lest they should perceive with their eyes and hear with their ears,
wistaklun blibbhon witipnon wasse innon.
and understand with their hearts and turn and I would heal them.'
dilkon den Tubaihon l'ainaikon dxazyan widnaikon dSam'an.
But blessed are your eyes for they see and your ears for they hear.
amen ger amar-na lkon dsaggiye nbiyye wzaddiqe
Truly I say to you, many prophets and just men
itragragu dyexzon middem dxazein-tton wla xazau
longed to see what you see, and did not see it,
walmiSma' middem dSam'in-tton wla Sma'u.
and to hear what you hear and did not hear it.

The sower explained

Mt13,18 M4,13 L8,11

atton den Sma'u matla dzar'a
But hear the parable of the sower.
koll dSama' millta dmalkuta wla mistakkal bah
Whoever hears the word of the kingdom and does not understand it
ate biSa wxaTep millta dazri'a blibbeh
the evil one comes and snatches the word sown in his heart,
hanaw-u d'al yad urxa izdra'.
this is what was sown beside the road.
haw den d'al So'a izdra' haw-u dSama' millta
And that which was sown on the rocks is he who hears the word
wbar Sa'teh bxaduta mqabbel lah
and at once with joy accepts it.
layt leh den 'iqqara bah ella dzabna-w.
but it has no root in him, except for a while.
wma dahawa ulcana aw rdupya miTTol millta
and when there is trouble or persecution on account of the word,
'agal mitkSel.
at once he falls away.
haw den dbeit kubbe izdra' haw-u dSama' millta
Now that which was sown among thorns is he who hears the word,

wrenya d'alma hana wTu'yai d'utra
but the cares of this world and the deception of riches
xanqin lah lmillta wadla pere hawya.
choke the word and becomes without fruit.
haw den d'al ar'a Tabta izdra' haw-u dSama' millati
Now that which was sown in good soil is he who hears my word
wmistakkal wyaheb pere
and understands it and bears fruit
w'abed it dama' wit diStin wit datlatin.
and yields a hundred, or sixty or thirty-fold.

Parable of the seed

M4,26-29

hakanna-y malkuta dalaha ak naS dyarme zar'a bar'a
The kingdom of God is as if one would scatter seed on the soil
widmak waiqum blilya wabimama
and would sleep and rise night and day
wzar'a irbe wyerak kad hu la yada'.
and the seed would sprout and grow, while is not aware.
ar'a ger maitya leh lpera wluqdam hawe 'esba
The earth yields fruit of itself and first comes the stalk,
wbatreh Sibla xrayat den xiTTa mSamlaita bSibla.
then the ear and finally the full grain in the ear.
ma daSmen den pera mixda atya maggla
When the fruit is ripe, at once comes the sickle,
dmaTTi xacada.
because the harvest has arrived.

The parable of the weeds

Mt13,24-30

damya malkuta daSmaiya lgabra dazra'
The kingdom of heaven is like a man who sowed
zara' Taba baqritah wkad dmeku naSa
good seed in his field, but while people slept
etta b'eldbabeh wzra' zizane bainat xiTTe wezal.
his enemy came and sowed weeds among the wheat and went off.
kad den i'a 'isba wa'abad pere
But when the blade sprouted and bore grain,
haiden itixziyu ap zizane.
the the weeds appeared also.
waqrebu 'abadawhi dmare baita wameru leh:
And the servants of the master of the house came and said to him:
maran la ha zara' Taba zra't baqritak?
'Master, did you not sow good seed in your field?

min aimekka it beh zizane?
From where are the weeds in it?'
hu den amar lhon: gabra b'eldbaba 'abad hade.
And he said to them: 'An enemy has done this.'
amrin leh 'abdawhi:
The servants said to him:
cabe att yezal igabbe innon?
'Do you want us to go and pick them out?'
hu den amar lhon:
But he said to them:
dalma kad mgabbein atton zizane
'No, lest while you are picking out the weeds,
ti'iqrun 'ammhon ap xiTTe.
you may uproot the wheat with them.'
Sboqu rabein traihon akda 'adamma laxacada:
Let both grow together until the harvest,
wabzabna daxacada amar-na lxacode:
and at the harvest time I will tell the reapers:
gabbau luqdam zizane wassoru innon mesaryata dyeqdun
Pick out weeds first and bind them in bundles to be burned
xiTTe den kanneSu innen lawcrai.
but gather the wheat into my barns.

The parable of the mustard seed
Mt13,31 M4,30
damya malkuta daSmaiya lapridta dxardla
The kingdom of heaven is like a grain of mustard seed
dansab gabra zara' baqriteh.
which a man took and sowed in his field.
whi z'orya-y min kullhon zar'one ma den darbat
And it is smaller than all other seeds but when it is grown,
rabba-y min kullhon yarkone whawya ilana
it is larger than all of the herbs and becomes a tree,
ak dtete paraxta daSmaiya taqqen bsawkeh.
so that the birds of the sky come and nest in its branches.

The parable of the leaven
Mt13,33 L13,20

damya malkuta daSmaiya laxamira haw dSiqlat attta
The kingdom of heaven is like yeast which a woman took,
Timrat batlat s'in dqamxa
mixed in with three measures of flour
'adamma dkulleh xama'.
until all of it was leavened.

The weeds explained

Mt13,37-43

haw dazra' zar'a Taba itawhi breh dnaSa
He who sows the good seed is the Son of man,
waqrita iteh 'alma:
the field is the world,
zara' den Taba bneih innon dmalkuta
and the good seed are the sons of the kingdom,
zizane den itaihon bnawhi dbiSa
and the weeds are the sons of the evil one,
b'eldbaba den dazra' innon itawhi saTana.
and the enemy who sowed them is the devil.
xacada den itawhi Sulameh d'alma
The harvest is the end of the world
xacode den malake.
and the reapers are angels.
aikanna hakel dmitgabbein zizane wyaqdin bnura
So just as the weeds are gathered up and burned with fire.
hakanna ihwe bSulameh d'alma hana.
so it will be at the end of this world.
iSaddar breh dnaSa malakawhi
The Son of man will send his angels
waigabbon min malkuteh kullhon makSule
and they will pick out of his kingdom all who offend
wkullhon 'abdai 'awla wyarmon innon battona dnura
and all evildoers and will throw them into the furnace of fire,
tamman ihwe bikya wxuraq Sinne.
and there will be wailing and gnashing of teeth.
haiden zaddiqe inihrun ak SimSa
Then the just will shine like the sun
bmalkuteh dabukon.
in the kingdom of their Father.
man dit leh idne diSma' iSma'!
He who has ears to hear, let him hear!

The parable of a hidden treasure

Mt13,44

tub damya malkuta daSmaiya lsimta damTaSya baqrita
Again the kingdom of heaven is like a treasure hidden in a field,
hai deSkxah gabra wTaSyah
which a man found and hid it,
wmin xaduteh ezal zabben koll dit leh
and from joy over it, he went and sold everything he had
wzabnah laqrita hai.
and bought that field.

The parable of the pearl

Mt13,45-46

tub damya malkuta daSmaiya lgabra taggara
Again, the kingdom of heaven is like a merchant
dba'e wa marganyata Tabata
who was seeking fine pearls
kad den eSkax marganita xada yaqqirat dmaiya
and when he had found one pearl of great value,
ezel zabben koll ma dit leh wzabnah.
he went, sold all that he had and bought it.

The parable of the net

Mt13,47-50

tub damya malkuta daSmaiya lamcidta
Again, the kingdom of heaven is like a net
dniplat byamma wmin koll gnes kanSat.
which was cast into the sea and caught all kinds of fish.
wkad mlat askuh lasparai yamma
When it was full, they drew it ashore,
witebu gabbiyu
sat down to sort them,
wTabe armiyu bmane wbiSa Sdau lbar.
and they put the good into baskets and the bad threw out.
hakanna ihwe bSulameh d'alma:
So it will be at the end of the world,
ippqun malake waiparSun
the angels will come out and separate
biSe min bainai zaddiqe
the evil from among the just,
wyarmon innon battona dnura:
and throw them into the furnace of fire;
tamman ihwe bikya wxuraq Sinne.
there shall be wailing and gnashing of teeth.

Treasures new and old

Mt13,51-53

istakkalton kullhen halen?
Have you understood all this?
miTTol hana koll sapra dmittalmad lmalkut Smaiya
Therefore every scribe instructed for the kingdom of heaven
dame lgabra mare baita
is like the master of the house
dmappeq min simateh xadtata w'attiqata.
who brings out of his treasure things new and old.

62

The healing at the pool

J5,6-14

cabe att dtitxlem?
Do you want to be healed?
qum Sqol 'arsak whallek!
Rise, take up your bed and walk!
ha xalim att: tub la texTe
Look, you are well, do not sin anymore,
dalma ihwe lak middem dbiS min qadmaya.
lest should happen to you something worse than before.

The work of the Son

J5,17-24

abi 'adamma lahaSa 'abed: ap ana 'abed-na.
My Father is working still, and I also am working.
amen amen amar-na Ikon:
Truly, truly I tell you:
dla miSkax bra 'abed middem min cbut napSeh
the Son cannot do anything on his own
ella middem dxaze laba d'abed.
but only what he sees the Father doing.
ailen ger daba 'abed halen ap bra akwateh 'abed.
For what the Father does, these things the Son does likewise.
aba ger raxem labreh
For the Father loves his Son
wkoll middem d'abed mxawwe leh
and everything that he does, shows to him
wadyattirin min halen 'abade mxawwe leh
and greater works than these he will show to him,
datton titdamrun.
so that you will marvel.
aikanna ger daba mqim mite wmaxe lhon
For as the Father raises the dead and gives them life,
hakanna ap bra lailen dcabe maxe.
so also the Son to whom he wishes gives life.
la wa ger aba da'en InaS
Nor does the Father judge anyone,
ella kulleh dina yahbeh labra:
but all judgment has given to the Son,
dkoll naS yaqqar labra ak damyaqqar laba.
that all may honor the Son just as they honor the Father.
haw dla myaqqar labra
He who does not honor the Son,
la myaqqar laba dSaddreh.
does not honor the Father who sent him.

64

amen amen amar-na lkon dman Sama' millati
Truly, truly I tell you, he who hears my word
waihaimen lman dSaddrani it leh xaiye dal'alam
and believes him who sent me has eternal life and
waldina la ate ella Sanni leh min mawta lxaiye.
does not come to judgment but has passed from death to life.

Two resurrections
J5,25-29
amen amen amarna lkon datya Sa'ta ap haSa iteh
Truly, truly I tell you, the hour is coming and now is,
emmati dmite iSm'un qaleh dabreh dalaha
when the dead will hear the voice of the Son of God,
whanon dSam'in ixxon.
and those who hear will live.
aikanna ger dlaba it xaiye baqnomeh
For just as the Father has life in himself,
hakanna yab ap labra dihwon xaiye baqnomeh
so he gave to the Son also to have life in himself
waSalTeh dihwe 'abed ap dina
and he gave him power to exercise judgment
dabreh-u den dnaSa.
because he is the Son of man.
la titdamrun bhade datya Sa'ta
Do not marvel at this, for an hour is coming
emmati dkullhon ailen dabqabre innon
when all who are in the tombs
iSm'un qaleh wippqun:
will hear his voice and will come out -
ailen da'abadu Tabata laqyamta dxaiye
those who have done good, to the resurrection of life,
wailen da'badu biSata
and those who have done evil,
laqyamta ddina.
to the resurrection of judgment.

Witnesses to Jesus
J5,30-40
la miSkax-na min cbut napSi middem lme'bbad.
I cannot by myself do anything.
ella aikanna dSama'-na da'en-na wdini zaddiq-u:
But as I hear, I judge, and my judgment is just,
la ger ba'e-na cibyani
because I do not seek my will
ella cibyaneh dman dSaddrani.
but the will of him who sent me.

65

in ana mashed-na 'al napSi sahaduti la hawat Sarrira.
If I testify about myself, my testimony is not true.
xren-u haw dmashed 'alai
But there is another who testifies of me
wyada'-na dSarrira-y sahaduteh dmashed 'alai
and I know that his testimony is true which he gives about me.
atton Saddarton lwat yoxannan washed 'al Srara
You sent to John and he has testified to truth.
ella den la wa min barnaSa naseb-na sahadut
However, from humans I do not accept testimony
ella halen amar-na datton tixxon.
but this I am saying that you may be saved.
haw Sraga wa ddaleq wmanhar
He was a lamp that was burning and shining,
cbaiton dtiStabharun dSa'ta bnuhareh.
you were willing to rejoice for a while in his light.
li den it li sahaduta drabba min dyoxannan
But I have testimony greater than John's,
'abade ger dyab li abi deSallem innon:
for the works which my Father has given me to accomplish -
hinnon 'abade d'abed-na sahadin 'alai
these works that I do - testify about me
daba Salxani.
that the Father has sent me.
waba dSalxani hu sahed 'alai.
And the Father who sent me, he has testified of me.
la qaleh min mtom Sma'ton wla xecweh xazaiton.
His voice you have never heard nor his form you have seen.
wmillteh la mqawya bkon:
And his word does not abide in you,
miTTol dabhaw dhu Saddar atton la mhaihmnin-tton.
because in him whom he sent you do not believe.

Witness of the Scripture

J5,39-47

bcau ktabe dabhon msabrin-tton
You search the scriptures, because you think that in them
dxaiye dal'alam it lkon.
you have eternal life.
whinnon sahadin 'alai
It is these that testify about me,
wla cabein atton dteton lwati
yet you are unwilling to come to me
dxaiye dal'alam ihwon lkon.
that you may have eternal life.

Subxa min bnainaSa la naseb-na
Glory from human beings I do not accept,
ella ida'tkon dxubbeh dalaha lait bkon.
but I know that you do not have love of God in you.
ana etteit baSmeh dabi wla mqabblin-tton li
I have come in my Father's name, and you do not accept me,
in xren yete bSem napSeh lhaw tqabblin.
if another comes in his own name, you will accept him.
aikanna miSkxin-tton lamhaimanu
How can you believe,
dSubxa xad min xad mqabblin-tton
when you accept glory from one another
wSubxa dmin xad alaha la ba'ein-tton.
and the glory which comes from the only God you do not seek.
lma sabrin-tton dana mqaTreg-na Ikon qdam aba.
Do not think that I will accuse you before the Father.
itawhi man damqaTreg Ikon muSe
The one who will accuse you is Moses,
haw dbeh sabbarton.
in whom you have placed your hope.
illu ger bmuSe haimenton ap bi mhaimnin waiton:
For if you believed Moses, you also would believe me,
muSe ger 'alai ktab.
for Moses wrote about me.
win laktabawhi dhaw la mhaimnin-tton
But if his writings you do not believe,
aikanna lmillai dili thaimnun?
how will you believe my words?

Five thousand fed

J6,5-12 Mt14,16 M6,38

aimikka nizbben laxma dyeklun halen?
Where are we to buy bread for these people to eat?
la mitb'e lhon lmezal: habu lhon atton lmekal.
They do not have to go, you give the something to eat.
zelu xazau kma laxmin it Ikon harka.
Go and see, how many loaves you have here.
aittau innon li harka!
Bring them here to me!
'abedu naSa kullhon distamkun!
Make the people sit down!
kanneSu qcaye ditaru
Gather up the fragments left over,
dla yebad middem.
so that nothing may be lost.

67

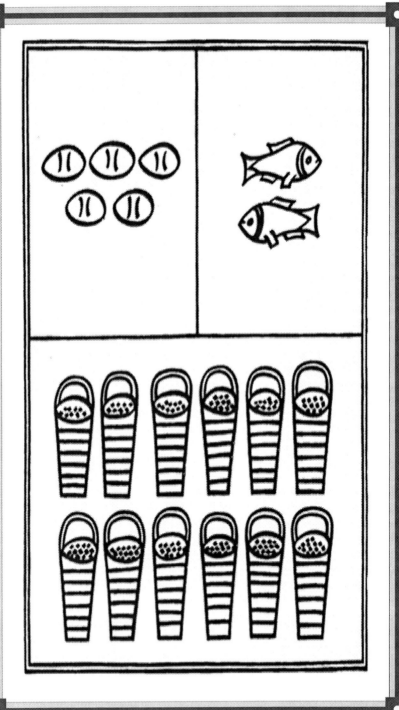

The Bread of Life

J6,26-36

amen amen amar-na Ikon
Truly, truly I tell you,
dba'ein-tton li la wa miTTol daxazaiton atwata
you are looking for me, not because you saw signs,
ella dekalton laxma wasba'ton.
but because you ate the loaves and were filled.
la tipilxun mekulta dabda
Do not work for the food that perishes,
ella mekulta damqawya lxaiye dal'alam:
but for the food which endures to eternal life,
aida dabreh dnaSa itten Ikon
which the Son of man will give to you,
lhana ger aba xatam alaha.
for it is on him that the Father, God, has set his seal.
hana-w 'abada dalaha dathaimnun bman dhu Saddar.
This is the work of God, that you believe in him whom he sent.
amen amen amar-na Ikon:
Truly, truly I tell you,
dla wa muSe yab Ikon laxma min Smaiya
it is not Moses who gave you bread from heaven,
ella abi yaheb Ikon laxma dquSta min Smaiya
but it is my Father who gives you the true bread from heaven.
laxma ger dalaha itawhi haw danxet min Smaiya
For the bread of God is that which comes down from heaven
wyaheb xaiye l'alma.
and gives life to the world.
ana-na laxma dxaiye.
I am the bread of life.
man date lwati la ikpan
He who comes to me will not hunger,
wman damhaimen bi la iche l'alam.
and he who believes in me will never thirst.
ella emret Ikon daxazaitonani wla mhaimnin atton.
But I said to you that you have seen me and yet do not believe.

The will of the Father

J6,37-46

koll dyab li abi lwati yete
All that my Father gives me will come to me
wman dalwati yete la appqeh lbar.
and him who comes to me I will not cast out.
dnixtet min Smaiya la de'bbed cibyani
For I have come down from heaven not to do my own will,

ella de'bbed cibyaneh dman dSaddrani.
but to do the will of him who sent me.
hana hu ger cibyaneh dman dSaddrani
This is the will of him who sent me
dkoll dyab li la awbed minneh
that of all that he has given me I should lose nothing,
ella aqqimiwhi byawma xraya.
but raise it up on the last day.
hana-w ger cibyaneh dabi
For this is the will of my Father
dkol dxaze labra waihaimen beh
that everyone who sees the Son and believes in him
ihwon leh xaiye dal'alam
should have eternal life,
wana aqqimiwhi byawma xraya.
and I will raise him up on the last day.
la tirTnun xad 'am xad.
Do not grumble among yourselves.
la naS miSkax dyete lwati
No one can come to me
ella in nagdeh aba dSaddrani
unless the Father who sent me draws him
wana aqqimiwhi byawma xraya.
and I will raise him up on the last day.
ktib ger banbiyye: dihwon kullhon malpe dalaha.
It is written in the prophets: 'They shall all be taught by God.'
koll man dSama' hakel min aba
So everyone who has heard from the Father
wyalep minneh ate lwati.
and learned from him comes to me.
la wa dxaze naS laba ella man dmin alaha itawhi
No one has seen the Father except the one who is from God,
haw-u xaze laba.
he has seen the Father.

I am the Bread of Life

J6,47-58

amen amen amar-na lkon
Truly, truly I tell you,
dman damhaimen bi it leh xaiye dal'alam.
he who believes in me, has eternal life.
ana-na laxma dxaiye.
I am the bread of life.
abahaikon ekalu manna bmadbra wmitu.
Your fathers ate the manna in the wilderness, and they died.

70

hana-w den laxma danxet min Smaiya
This is the bread that comes down from heaven
dyekol naS minneh wla imut.
so that one may eat of it and not die.
ana-na laxma dxaiye dmin Smaiya nixtet:
I am the living bread that came down from heaven;
win naS yekol min hana laxma ixxe l'alam wlaxma
whoever eats of this bread will live forever, and the bread
aina dana etten pagri-w d'al appai xaiyawhi d'alma yaheb-na.
that I will give is my flesh for the life of the world.
amen amen amar-na Ikon din la teklun pagreh dabreh dnaSa
Truly, truly I tell you, unless you eat the flesh of the Son of man
wtiSton dmeh lait Ikon xaiye baqnomkon.
and drink his blood, you have no life in yourselves.
man dakel den min pagri wSate min demi
He who eats my flesh and drinks my blood
it leh xaiye dal'alam wana aqqimiwhi byawma xraya.
has eternal life, and I will raise him up at the last day.
pagri ger Sarrira'it itawhi mekulta
For my flesh is true food
wdemi Sarrira'it itawhi miStya.
and my blood is true drink.
man dakel pagri wSate demi bi mqawwe wana beh.
He who eats my flesh and drinks my blood abides in me and I in him.
aikanna dSaddrani aba xaiya wana xai-na miTTol aba:
As the living Father sent me and I live because of the Father,
wman dyeklani ap hu ixxe miTTolati.
so he who eats me will live because of me.
hana-w laxma danxet min Smaiya
This is the bread which came down from heaven,
la wa ak dekalu abahaihon manna wmitu
not as your fathers ate manna and died,
man dekal hana laxma ixxe l'alam.
he who eats this bread will live forever.

The words of spirit and life

                    J6,60-71

hade makiSla Ikon?
Does this offend you?
in texzon hakel labreh dnaSa
Then if you were to see the Son of man
dsaleq lattar ditawhi wa min qdim?
ascending to where he was before?
ruxa-y dmaxya: pagra la mahane middem.
It is the spirit that gives life; the flesh profits nothing.

71

mille dana mallet 'ammkon ruxa innen wxaiye innen:
The words that I have spoken to you are spirit and life,
ella it naSa minnkon dla mhaimnin.
but there are some of you that do not believe.
miTTol hana emret Ikon dla naS miSkax dyete lwati
This is why I told you that no one can come to me,
in la ihib leh min abi.
unless it is given him by my Father.
Ima ap atton cbein-tton Imezal?
Do you also wish to go away?
la wa ana gbeitkon latre'sar wminnkon xad saTana-w.
Did I not choose you, the twelve? Yet one of you is a devil.

To the Pharisees on tradition
Mt15,3-20 M7,1-23
Imana ap atton 'abrin-tton 'al puqdana dalaha
And why do you transgress the commandment of God
miTTol maSelmanutkon?
for the sake of your tradition?
alaha ger emar: yaqqar labuk wlimmak
For God commanded: 'Honor your father and your mother
wman damcaxxe labuhi wlimmeh mmat imut.
and who curses his father or his mother shall die.'
atton den amrin-tton: koll man dyemar laba aw limma:
But you say: 'Whoever tells his father or his mother,
qurbani middem dtitihne menni
it is my offering what you would have gained from me,
wla yaqqar labuhi aw limmeh.
then he need not honor his father or mother.'
wbaTTelton millta dalaha miTTol maSelmanutkon.
So you made void the word of God for the sake of your tradition.
nasbai bappe: Sappir itnabbi 'alaikon eSa'ya nbiyya wemar:
Hypocrites, well did the prophet Isaiah prophesy about you saying:
'amma hana bsepwateh hu myaqqar li:
'This people honors me with their lips,
libbhon den saggi raxxiq menni wasriq'ait daxlin li.
but their hearts are far from me, in vain do they worship me,
kad mallpin yulpane dpuqdana dabnainaSa.
when they teach as doctrines the precepts of men.'
Sma'u wistakkalu!
Listen and understand!
la wa middem d'a'el lpuma msaiyeb IbarnaSa
It is not what goes into the mouth that defiles a person
ella middem dnapeq min puma haw-u msaiyeb IbarnaSa.
but it is what comes out of the mouth that defiles one.

koll necebbta aida dla nacbbah abi dbaSmaiya tit'aqar.
Every plant that my Father in heaven did not plant will be uprooted.
Sboqu lhon: smaiya innon nagode dasmaiya.
Let them alone, they are blind guides of the blind.
samya den Isamya in idabbar traihon bgumca naplin.
If a blind person leads a blind person, both will fall into a pit.
'adamma lhaSa ap atton la mistakklin-tton?
Even you still do not understand?
la yad'in-tton dmiddem d'a'el lpuma
Do you not know that whatever goes into the mouth
lkarsa-w azel wmin tamman btadkita miStde lbar:
enters the stomach, and from there passes into the latrine;
middem den dmin puma napeq min libba napeq
but what comes out of the mouth comes out from the heart,
whuyu msaiyeb leh IbarnaSa.
and this is what defiles a person.
min lagaww ger min libba dabnainaSa napqan maxSbata
For from within, out of the heart of person come evil
biSata gawra qiTla zanyuta gannabuta sahadut Suqra:
thoughts, adultery, murder, fornication, theft, false witness,
'alobuta biSuta nikla caxnuta 'aina biSta gudapa
avarice, wickedness, deceit, licentiousness, envy, slander,
Sabharanuta SaTyuta.
pride, folly.
halen kullhen biSata min lgaww-u napqan
All these evil things come from within
wamsaiyban leh IbarnaSa:
and they defile a person,
in naS den il'as kad la mSagan idawhi la mistaiyab.
but to eat with unwashed hands does not defile.

The Canaanite woman
Mt15,24-28 M7,24-30
la iStaddret ella lwat 'erbe daT'au min beit israyel.
I was sent only to the lost sheep of the house of Israel.
la Sappir Imissab laxma dabnaiya walmarmayu Ikalbe.
It is not fair to take the children's bread and throw it to the dogs.
o attta rabba-y haimanuteki!
Oh woman, great is your faith!
ihwe leki ak dcabya atti.
Let it be done for you as you wish.
zeli miTTol hade millta:
You may go, because of this answer:
npaq leh Seda min barteki.
the demon has gone from your daughter.

73

Four thousand fed

Mt15,32-34 M6,31-38

taw Ikon yezal Idabra balxodain witnixi qallil.
Come away by yourselves to a lonely place and rest a while.

mitraxam-na 'al kinSa hana dha tlata yawmin qawwiyu Iwati
I pity this crowd, for it is three days they remained with me

wlait lhon ma dyeklun:
and they have nothing to eat,

udeSre innon kad caiyamin la cabe-na
and to send them away while fasting I do not want,

dalma i'upun burxa.
for they might faint on the way.

kma laxmin it Ikon?
How many loaves do you have?

The walking on the water

Mt14,27-31 M6,50 J6,20

itlabbabu! ana-na la tedexlun!
Take courage! That is me, do not be afraid!

ta!
Come!

z'or haimanuta Imana itpallagt?
You of little faith, why did you doubt?

The healing of the deaf man

M7,34

itpattax!
Ephphatha—be opened!

The Pharisees demand for a sign

Mt16,2-4 L12,54-56

ma dahawa ramSa amrin atton:
When it is the evening, you say:

caxwa-w simqat ger Smaiya.
It will be clear, for the sky is red.

wabcapra amrin atton:
And in the morning you say:

yawmana satwa-w simqat ger Smaiya kmira'it.
Today it will be stormy for the sky is red and gloomy.

ma xazaiton 'anana ddanxa min ma'arba mixda amrin:
When you see the cloud rising in the west, you say at once:

miTra ate: whawa hakanna.
A shower is coming. And so it happens.

wma dnaSba taimna amrin-tton:
And when the south wind is blowing, you say:

75

xumma hawe whawe.
It will be hot day. And it happens.
nasbai bappe!
You hypocrites!
parcopa dar'a wadSmaiya yad'in-tton dtiperSun
The appearance of earth and sky you know how to interpret,
atwata dzabna hana la yad'in-tton dtiperSun.
but the signs of the present time you do not know how to interpret.
Sarbta biSta wgaiyarta ata ba'ya:
An evil and adulterous generation asks for a sign,
wata la mityaba lah ella in ateh dyawnan nbiyya.
and no sign shall be given it except the sign of Jonah the prophet.

The leaven of the Pharisees

Mt16,6-11

xazau izdahhru min xamira dapriSe wadzadduqaye.
Watch out and beware of the leaven of Pharisees and Sadducees.
mana mitxaSSbin-tton bnapSkon z'orai haimanuta
Why do you discuss among yourselves, you of little faith
dlaxma la Sqalton?
that you have no bread?
la 'adamma lhaSa istakkalton la 'ahaddin-tton
Do you still not understand and do you not remember
lhanon xammSa laxmin dxammSa alpin
the five loaves of the five thousand
wkama qopinon Sqalton?
and how many baskets you gathered?
wla lhanon Sab'a laxmin darb'a alpin
Or the seven loaves of the four thousand
wkama aspridin Sqalton?
and how many baskets you gathered?
aikanna la istakkalton
How is it that you do not understand
dla wa 'al laxma emret lkon
that I was not talking to you about bread
ella dtizdaharun min xamira dapriSe wadzadduqaye?
but to beware if the leaven of the Pharisees and Sadducees?

The blind man at Bethsaida

M8,23-26

mana xaze att?
Do you see anything?
apla laqrita te"ol!
Do not even enter the village!

76

Peter's confession

Mt16,13-20 M8,27 L9,18

mannu amrin 'alai ditai breh dnaSa?
Who do people say about me that the Son of man is?
atton den mannu amrin-tton ditai?
But you, who do you say that I am?
Tubaik Sim'on breh dyona!
Blessed are you, Simon son of Jonah!
dbisra wadma la gla lak
For flesh and blood has not revealed this to you,
ella abi dbaSmaiya.
but my Father who is in heaven.
ap ana amar-na lak: datt-u kepa
And I tell you: You are Kephas the Rock,
w'al hade kepa ebneh l'eddati
and upon this rock I will build my church
wtar'e daSyol la ixisnunah.
and the gates of Hades shall not prevail against it.
lak etten qlide dmalkuta daSmaiya
I will give you the keys of the kingdom of heaven,
wkoll middem dtesor bar'a
and whatever you bind on earth
ihwe assir baSmaiya:
shall be bound in heaven,
wmiddem dtiSre bar'a
and whatever you loose on earth
ihwe Sre baSmaiya.
shall be loosed in heaven.

The first prediction of the passion

L9,22 Mt16,21 M8,31

d'atid-u breh dnaSa dyezal loriSlem dsaggiyata yexaS
The Son of man must go to Jerusalem and suffer many things
wistle min qaSSiSe wrabbai kahane wsapre
and be rejected by the elders and chief priests and scribes,
wiqiTlunani walyawma datlata iqum.
and to be killed, and on the third day be raised.

A rebuke to Peter

Mt16,23 M8,33

zel lak lbestari saTana! tuqilta att li:
Get behind me, Satan! You are a hindrance to me,
dla mitra'e att dalaha ella dabnainaSa.
for you are not thinking of God but of men.

77

Mt16,24-28 M8,34-38 L9,23-27

man dcabe dyete batari ikpor bnapSeh
Whoever wishes to come after me must deny himself,
wiSqol zqipeh wyete batari.
and take up his cross and follow me.
man dcabe ger dyaxxe napSeh yawbdih
For whoever wishes to save his life will lose it
wman yawbed napSeh miTTolati
and he who loses his life for my sake
wmiTTol sbarti yaxxeih.
and the gospel's sake will save it.
mana ger itihne barnaSa in kulleh 'alma iqne
For what will it profit a man if he gains the whole world
wnapSeh ixsar?
and loses his soul?
aw man itten barnaSa taxlupa dnapSeh?
Or what will a man give in exchange for his soul?
koll ger dibhat bi wabmillay
For whoever is ashamed of me and of my words
bSarbta hade xaTTaita wgaiyarta
in this sinful and adulterous generation,
wap breh dnaSa ibhat beh
also the Son of man will be ashamed of him,
ma date bSubxa dabuhi 'am malakawhi qaddiSe
when he comes in the glory of his Father with his holy angels,
whaiden ipro' lnaS naS ak 'abadawhi.
and then he will repay every man according to his deeds.
amen amar-na lkon dit naSa dqaimin tnan
Truly, I tell you, there are some of those standing here
dla iT'amun mawta 'adamma dyexzon labreh dnaSa
who will not taste death until they see the Son of man
date bmalkuteh.
coming in his kingdom.

The Transfiguration

Mt17,1-9 M9,2-10 L9,28-36

qumu la tidixlun!
Get up! Do not be afraid!
l'ein naS la temrun xezwa hana
Tell no one about this vision,
'adamma daiqum breh dnaSa min mite.
until the Son of man is raised from the dead.

The coming of Elias

eliyya ate luqdam dkoll middem yatqqen.
Elias does come first to restore all things.
waikanna ktib 'al breh dnaSa
And how is it written about the Son of man
dsaggi yexxaS wistle?
that he must suffer greatly and be rejected?
ella amar-na lkon: dha eliyya etta
But I tell you that Elias has already come
wla yad'uhi
and they did not know him
wa'abadu beh kollma dacbaw
and did to him all what they wanted,
aikanna daktib 'alawhi.
as it is written about him.
hakanna ap breh dnaSa 'atid dyexxaS minnhon.
So also the Son of man must suffer from them.

The demoniac boy

Mt17,17-21 M9,16 L9,41

[To the crowd]
mana darSin atton 'ammhon?
What are you discussing with them?
on Sarbta dla mhaimna wam'aqalta
O faithless and perverse generation,
'adamma lemmati ehwe lwatkon?
how much longer must I be with you?
wa'adamma lemmati essaibarkon?
How much longer must I put up with you?
aitawhi li lka!
Bring him here to me!
[To boy's father]
dakma leh zabna ha min dhakanna-w?
How long has this been happening to him?
in miSkax att dathaimen?
If you can believe?
koll middem miSkax lman damhaimen.
All things are possible to him who believes.
[To the spirit]
ruxa xarSta dla mmalla ana paqed-na leki
You dumb and deaf spirit, I command you,
poqi minneh wtub la te"allin leh!
come out of him and again do not enter him!

The power of faith

[His disciples: 'Why we could not cast it out?']
miTTol la haimanutkon: amen ger amar-na Ikon
Because of your unbelief, for truly I say to you,
din tihwe bkon haimanuta ak pridta dxardla
if you have faith as a grain of mustard seed,
temrun lTura hana: dSanna mikka!
you will say to this mountain: 'Move from here!'
waySanne wmiddem la ixsankon.
and it will move and nothing will prevail over you.
hana den ginsa la napeq ella bcawma wbaclota.
But this kind does not go out except by fasting and prayer.

The second prediction of the passion

Mt17,22 M9,30 L9,44

simu atton mille halen bidnaikon!
Let these words sink into your ears!
'atid-u breh dnaSa diStlem bidai bnainaSa
The Son of man is going to be delivered into the hands of men
wiqiTlunaihi walyawma datlata iqum.
and they will kill him and on the third day he will rise.

Temple tax

Mt17,24-27

mana mitixze lak Simon?
What do you think, Simon?
malke dar'a min man nasbin maksa waksep reSa
The kings of the earth, from whom do they take toll and head tax,
min bnaihon aw min nukraye?
from their sons or from strangers?
[Peter answered: 'From strangers.']
maden bnai xere innon bnaiya.
Then the sons are free.
dla den yakSel innon zel lyamma
But so that we do not offend them, go to the sea
warma ballu'a wnuna qadmaya dsaleq
and cast the hook, and the first fish that comes up,
ptax pumeh wtiSkax isteira:
open its mouth and you will find a shekel,
hai sab whab xalapai waxalapaik.
take that and give to them for me and for yourself.

81

To his unbelieving brothers

J7,6-9

zabni dili 'adamma lhana la mTa
My time has not yet come
zabnkon den dilkon bkoll 'iddan mTaiyab.
but your time is always ready.
la miSkax 'alma lmisnakon li den sane
The world cannot hate you, but it hates me
miTTol dana mashed-na 'alawhi da'abadawhi biSin innon.
because I testify against it that its works are evil.
atton saqu l'ad'eda hana ana la saleq-na haSa l'ad'eda hana
Go to the feast yourselves, I am not going to this feast,
miTTol dzabna dili la 'adakkel Slem.
for my time has not yet fully come.

The greatest

Mt18,1-5 M9,33-37 L9,46-48

amen amar-na lkon din la tithapkun wtihwon ak Tlaye
Truly I tell you, unless you change and become like children,
la te'alun lmalkuta daSmaiya.
you will not enter the kingdom of heaven.
man hakel dammakkek napSeh ak hana Talya
Whoever humbles himself like this child,
hu ihwe rabb bmalkuta daSmaiya.
he is the greatest in the kingdom of heaven.
wman damqabbel ak Talya hana bSemi li-w mqabbel
Whoever welcomes one such child in my name welcomes me, and
wman dli mqabbel la-w li mqabbel ella lman dSaddrani.
whoever welcomes me does not welcome me but him who sent me.
ayna ger daz'or bkullkon hana ihwe rabb.
For he who is least among you all - he is the greatest.

The exorcist

M9,38 L9,49 Mt10,43

la tiklunaihi: lait ger naS d'abed xaile bSemi
Do not stop him, for there is no one who does deeds in my name
wmiSkax 'agal amar 'alay dbiS.
and is able right away to speak bad of me.
man dla wa hakel luqbalkon xlapaikon-u.
For he who is not against us is for us.
koll ger dyaSkeikon kasa dmaiya balxod baSma
Whoever gives you a cup of water only in the name
ddmaSixa atton: amen amar-na lkon dla yawbed agreh.
that you are Christ's, truly, I say to you he will not lose his reward.

82

Scandals

Mt18,6-10 M9,42 L17,1

wkoll dyakSel lxad min halen z'ore damhaimnin bi
and anyone who harms one of these little ones who believe in me,
paqqax-u leh dtihwe talya raxya daxamara bcawreh
it would be better for him to have a millstone hung around his neck
wamTabba b'umqawhi dyamma.
and be drowned into the depths of the sea.
wai l'alma min makSule!
Woe to the world because of scandals!
wale ger lyeton makSule
For it is necessary that scandals should come
wai den lgabra dbideh yeton makSule.
but woe to the man by whom scandals come.
in den idak aw riglak makiSla lak
And if your hand or foot offends you,
psoqeh waSdih minnak
cut it off and throw it away from you,
Tab-u lak ger dte"ol lxaiye kad xagis att aw kad pSig
for it is better for you to enter into life lame or maimed
wla kad it lak tartein idin aw tartein riglin
than having two hands or two feet
tippel bnura dal'alam.
to be thrown into eternal fire.
win hu d'ainak makiSla lak
And if your eye offends you,
xasih waSdih minnak
gouge it out and throw it away from you,
Tab-u lak dbaxada 'aina te'ol lxaiye
it is better for you with one eye to enter life
wla kad it lak tartein 'ainin tippel bgehanna dnura.
than having two eyes to be thrown into the hell of fire.
ayka dtawla'hon la maita wnurhon la da'ka.
where their worm does not die and their fire is not quenched.
xazaw la tibson 'al xad min halen z'ore:
See that you do not despise one of these little ones,
amar-na lkon ger dmalakaihon baSmaiya
for I tell you that their angels in heaven
bkullzban xazein parcopeh dabi dbaSmaiya.
always behold the face of my Father who is in heaven.
etta ger breh dnaSa dyaxxe middem dabbid wa:
For the Son of man has come to save what was lost.

The parable of the lost sheep

Mt18,12-14 L15,3-7

mana mitixze Ikon?
What do you think?
in ihwon InaS ma' 'erbin wyiT'e xad minnhon
If a man has a hundred sheep, and one of them goes astray,
la Sabeq tiS'in wtiS'a bTura
does he not leave the ninety-nine on the mountains
wazel ba'e Ihaw daT'a?
and go in search of the one that went astray?
win iSkexeh amen amar-na Ikon dxade beh
And if he finds it, I truly tell you, he rejoices over it
yattir min tiS'in wtiS'a dla T'au.
more than over the ninety-nine that did not stray.
xade wSaqel leh 'al katpateh wate Ibaita
Rejoicing he lays it on his shoulders, and coming home,
wqare raxmawhi wlaSbabawhi wamar Ihon:
he calls his friends and his neighbors telling them:
xadau 'ammi diSkxet 'irbi dabbid wa.
Rejoice with me for I have found my sheep which was lost.
amar-na Ikon dhakanna ihwe xaduta baSmaiya
Just so, I tell you, will be more joy in heaven
'al xad xaTTaya dta'eb aw 'al tiS'in wtiS'a zaddiqin
over one sinner who repents than over ninety-nine just
dla mitba'ya Ihon tyabuta.
who need no repentance.
hakanna lait cibyana qdam abi dbaSmaiya
So it is not the will of my Father who is in heaven
dyebad xad min halen z'ore.
that should perish one of these little ones.

A brother who sins

Mt18,15-18 L17,3

in den askel bak axuk zel akkessaihi
If your brother sins against you, go and show him his fault,
banaik wleh balxod.
between you and him alone.
in Sam'ak itart axuk.
If he listens to you, you have won your brother.
win la Sam'ak dbar 'ammak xad aw trein
If he does not listen, take one or two along with you,
d'al pum trein aw tlata sahaddin tqum koll milla.
for from the mouth of two or three witnesses stands every word.
in den apla Ihanon iSma' emar I'eddta.
If he then will not listen to them, tell it to the church.

84

in den apla l'eddta iSma'
If he does not listen even to the church,
ihwe lak ak maksa wak xanpa.
let him be to you as a tax collector and a Gentile.
wamen amar-na Ikon dkoll ma dtesrun bar'a
And truly I tell you, whatever you bind on earth
ihwe assir baSmaiya
will be bound in heaven
wmiddem dtiSron bar'a ihwe Sre baSmaiya.
and whatever you loose on earth will be loosed in heaven.
tub amar-na Ikon: din trein minnkon iStwon bar'a 'al koll cbu
Again I tell you, if two of you agree on earth about any desire
diSilun ihwe lhon min lwat abi dbaSmaiya:
they ask, it will be done for them by my Father in heaven.
aikanna ger datrein aw tlata kniSin bSemi
For where two or three are gathered in my name,
tamman-na bainathon.
I am there among them.

Forgiveness
Mt18,21 L17,4

la amar-na lak 'adamma laSba'
I do not say to you seven times,
ella 'adamma ISab'in zabnin Sba' Sba'.
but seventy times seven.

The parable of the unforgiving servant
Mt18,23-35

miTTol hana itdamyat malkuta daSmaiya lgabra malka
Therefore, the kingdom of heaven is likened to a king
dacba dissab xuSbana min 'abdawhi
who wished to settle accounts with his servants.
wkad Sarri lmessab qarrebu leh xad dxaiyab
When he began the reckoning, they brought to him one who owed
ribbon kakrin: wkad lait wa leh lmipra'
ten thousand talents; and as he could not pay,
pqad mareh dizdabban-u wattteh wbnawhi
his lord ordered him to be sold with his wife and children
wkoll middem dit leh wipro'.
and all that he had and payment to be made.
wanpal haw 'abda sged leh wemar:
So this servant fell down, bowed before him and said:
mari aggar 'alai ruxa wkoll middem para'-na lak.
'My lord, be patient with me and I pay you everything.'

witraxam mareh d'abda haw
And the lord had compassion of that servant
waSraihi wxawbteh Sbaq leh:
and released him and forgave him his debt.
npaq den 'abda haw weSkax lxad min knawateh
Then that servant went and found one of his fellow servants
dxaiyab wa leh deinare ma' waxdeh
who owed him a hundred denarii and seized him
wxaneq wa leh wamar leh:
and choked him saying to him:
hab li middem dxaiyab att li.
'Pay what you owe me.'
wanpal haw knateh 'al riglawhi b'a minneh wemar:
So his fellow servant fell down at his feet begging and said:
aggar 'alai ruxa wpara'-na lak.
'Be patient with me and I will repay you.'
hu den la cba ella ezal armyeh beit assire
But he was unwilling, but went and put him in prison
'adamma dintan leh ma dxaiyab leh.
until he would pay him what he owed him.
kad xazau den knawathon middem dahawa
When his fellow servants saw what happened,
keryat lhon Tab:
they were very sad;
wettau awwda'u lmarhon koll ma dahawa.
and they went and reported to their lord all that happened.
haiden qrayhi mareh wemar leh:
Then his lord called him and said to him:
'abda biSa: kullah xawbta Sibqet lak
'You evil servant, I forgave you all debt,
dab'ait minni:
because you begged me,
la wale wa lak ap att dtixxon laknatak
was it not right for you also to have mercy on your fellow servant
aikanna dana xantak?
as I had mercy on you?'
wargez mareh waSlemeh lamnagdane
And in anger his lord handed him over to the torturers
'adamma dipro' koll middem dxaiyab leh.
until he would pay him all he owed him.
hakanna ye'bbed lkon abi dbaSmaiya
So also will do to you my Father who is in heaven,
in la tiSbqun naS laxuhi
if each of you does not forgive his brother
min libbkon sakluteh.
from his heart his offenses.

The Festival of Tabernacles

J7,16-24

yulpani la wa dili ella dhaw dSaddrani.
My teaching is not mine, but his who sent me.

man dcabe dye'bbed cibyaneh mistakkal yulpani
If anyone is willing to do his will he will know my teaching

in min alaha-w aw ana min cbut napSi mmallel-na.
if it is from God or I from myself do speak.

man dmin cbut re'yaneh mmallel Subxa InapSeh ba'e
He who speaks from himself seeks his own glory,

haw den dSubxa dman Saddreh ba'e
but he who is seeking the glory of the one who sent him

Sarrir-u w'awla blibbeh la it.
is true and there is no wrong in his heart.

la wa muSe yab Ikon oraita?
Did not Moses give you the law?

wla naS minnkon naTar oraita.
Yet none of you keeps the law.

mana ba'ein-tton ImiqTlani?
Why do you seek to kill me?

xad 'abada 'ebdet wkullhon mittdamrin–tton.
I did one work and all of you are astonished.

miTTol hana muSe yab Ikon gzurta
For this reason Moses gave you circumcision,

la wa miTTol dminneh-i min muSe ella dmin ahabata-y
not that it is from him, from Moses, but from the patriarchs,

wabSabbta gazrin innon barnaSa.
and on the Sabbath you circumcise a man.

in barnaSa mitgezar byawma dSabbta
If a man is circumcised on the day of Sabbath,

miTTol dla iStre oraita dmuSe 'alay raTnin atton
so that the law of Moses may not be broken, are you angry with me

dkulleh barnaSa axalmet byawma dSabbta?
because the whole man I healed on the day of the Sabbath?

la tihwon daynin bmassab dappe ella dina kena dunu.
Do not judge by looks, but judge with right judgment.

I came from the Father

J7,28-38

wli yad'in-tton wmin aimikka-na yad'in-tton.
You know me and you know where I am from.

wmin cbut napSi la etteit ella Sarrir-u man dSaddrani
Yet I did not come on my own, but he is true who sent me

haw datton la yad'in-tton leh.
whom you do not know.

88

ana den yad'a-na leh dmin lwateh-na whu Saddrani.
I know him, for I am from him, and he sent me.
qallil tub zabna 'ammkon-na wazel-na lwat man dSaddrani.
A little while longer I am with you, then I go to him who sent me.
wtib'onani wla tiSkxunani.
You will look for me and you will not find me.
waika dana itay atton la miSkxin-tton lmeta.
And where I am, you cannot come.
in naS che yete lwati wiSte.
Let anyone who thirsts come to me and drink.
kollman damhaimen bi aikanna demaru ktabe:
Whoever believes in me, as scripture says:
naharawata dmaiya dxaiye irdon min karseh.
'Rivers of living water will flow from within him.'

The woman caught in adultery
J8,7-11

ayna minnkon ditawhi dla xaTa qadmaya iSde 'aleh kepa.
Who among you is without sin let him first throw a stone at her.
attta aika itayhon? la naS xaiyabeki?
Woman, where are they? Has no one condemned you?
apla ana mxaiyeb-na leki:
Neither do I condemn you.
zeli wmin haSa tub la texTen.
Go, and from now on do not sin again!

The Light of the world
J8,12-20

ana-na nuhreh d'alma:
I am the light of the world.
man dbatari ate la ihallek bxeSSoka
Whoever follows me will not walk in the darkness,
ella iSkax leh nuhara dxaiye.
but will have the light of life.
apin ana mashed-na 'al napSi Sarrira-y sahaduti
Even if I do testify on my own behalf, my testimony is true,
miTTol dyada'-na aimikka etteit wlaika azel-na:
because I know where I came from and where I am going.
atton den la yad'in-tton min aimikka etteit wla laika azel-na.
but you do not know where I come from or where I am going.
atton pagrana'it dainin-tton ana lnaS la da'en-na.
You judge according to the flesh, I judge no one.
win da'en-na den dini Sarrir-u
But even if I do judge, my judgment is true,

89

miTTol dla haweit balxodai ella ana wabi dSaddrani.
for I am not alone, but I and my Father who sent me.
wabnomoskon den ktib dsahaduta datrein gabrin Sarrira-y:
Even in your law it is written that a testimony of two men is true:
ana-na dsahed-na 'al napSi wabi dSaddrani sahed 'alay.
I testify on my behalf and my Father who sent me testifies about me.
wla li yad'in-tton wla labi:
You know neither me nor my Father.
illu li yad'in waiton ap labi yad'in waiton.
If you knew me, you would know my Father also.

The Father's Ambassador

J8,21-29

ana azel-na wtib'onani watmutun baxaTahaikon
I am going away and you will look for me, but you will die in your sin.
waika dana azel-na atton la miSkxin-tton Imeta.
Where I am going, you cannot come.
atton min daltaxt atton wana min dal'el-na:
You are from below, I am from above;
atton min hana atton 'alma ana la hawet min hana 'alma.
You are of this world, I am not of this world.
emret Ikon datmutun baxaTahaikon
I said to you that you will die in your sins,
in la ger thaimnun dana-na tmutun baxaTahaikon.
for unless you believe that I am he, you will die in your sins.
apin dSarrit demallel 'ammkon?
From the beginning what I have been telling you?
saggi it li 'alaikon Imemar wlammedan:
I have much to say about you and much to condemn;
ella man dSaddrani Sarrir-u
but he who sent me is true,
wana ailen dSim'et minneh halen-u mmallel-na b'alma.
and what I have heard from him, that I tell the world.
emmati datrimuneh la breh dnaSa
When you have lifted up the Son of man,
haiden tid'un dana-na wmiddem min cbut napSi la 'abed-na
then you will know that I am he and do nothing on my own
ella aikanna dallepani abi hakwat-u mmallel-na.
but as my Father taught me thus I speak.
wman dSaddrani 'ammi itawhi
And he who sent me is with me;
wla Sabqani balxodai abi:
and my Father has not left me alone,
miTTol dana middem dSapar leh 'abed-na bkollzban.
because what is pleasing to him I do all the time.

The truth will make you free

J8,31-36

in atton tkattrun bmillati Sarrira'it talmidai atton:
If you continue in my word, you are truly my disciples,
wtid'un Srara whu Srara ixarrarkon.
and you will know the truth, and the truth will make you free.
amen amen amar-na Ikon dkollman d'abed xaTita
Truly, truly I say to you everyone who commits sin
'abdah-u dxaTita.
is slave to sin.
w'abda la mqawwe l'alam bbaita:
The slave does not remain forever in the household
bra den l'alam mqawwe.
but the son forever remains.
in hu hakel dabra ixarrarkon Sarrira'it tihwon bnai xere.
So if the Son makes you free, then truly you will be free sons.

Children of the devil - To the Jews

J8,37-47

yada'-na dzar'eh atton dabraham.
I know that you are descendants of Abraham.
ella ba'ein-tton ImiqTlani miTTol dalmillati la sapqin-tton.
But you are trying to kill me, because my word has no room in you.
ana middem daxazeit lwat abi mmallel-na:
What I have seen with my Father I tell you,
watton middem daxazaiton lwat abukon 'abdin-tton.
and you, what you have seen from your father, you do.
illu bnawhi waiton dabraham 'abadawhi dabraham
If you were children of Abraham, the works of Abraham
'abdin waiton: haSa ha ba'ein-tton ImiqTlani
you would do, but now you are trying to kill me,
lgabra dSarrirta mallet 'ammkon aida dSim'et min alaha.
a man who has told you the truth that I heard from God.
hade abraham la 'abad.
This Abraham did not do.
atton den 'abdin-tton 'abade dabukon.
You are doing the works of your father.
illu alaha wa abukon mxabin waiton li
If God were your Father, you would love me,
ana ger min alaha nipqet wetteit.
for from God I proceeded and came.
wla wa min cbut napSi etteit ella hu Saddrani.
I did not come of my own accord, but he sent me.
miTTol mana millati la miStawd'in-tton?
Why you do not comprehend my word?

91

'al dla miSkxin-tton Sam'in millati.
It is because you cannot hear my word.
atton min aba akelqarca itaikon
You are from your father the devil,
wrigteh dabukon cabein-tton lme'bbad.
and the desires of your father you want to do.
haw dmin braSit qaTel naSa-w
he was from the beginning a mankiller,
wbaSrara la qa'em: miTTol daSrara lait beh.
and in truth he does not stand, because there is no truth in him.
wemmati dammallel kadabuta min dileh hu mmallel
When he tells a lie, he speaks from his own nature,
miTTol ddaggala-w ap abuh.
for he is a liar and the father of lies.
ana den daSrara mmallel-na la mhaimnin-tton li
But because I tell the truth, you do not believe me.
mannu minnkon makkes li 'al xaTita?
Which of you convicts me of sin?
win Srara mmallel-na atton lmana la mhaimnin-tton li?
If I tell the truth, why you do not believe me?
man dmin alaha itawhi mille dalaha Sama':
Whoever is from God hears the words of God.
miTTol hana atton la Sam'in-tton
For this reason you do not hear,
miTTol dla hawaiton min alaha.
because you are not from God.

Before Abraham was, I am
J8,49-59
li daiwa la it ella labi myaqqar-na watton mca'arin li.
I do not have a demon, but I honor my Father and you dishonor me.
ana den la ba'e-na Subxi: it-u dba'e wda'en.
I do not seek my glory, there is one who seeks it and he is the judge.
amen amen amar-na lkon dman dmillati naTar
Truly, truly I say to you, whoever keeps my word
mawta la yexze l'alam.
will never see death.
in ana mSabbax-na napSi Subxi la hawa middem:
If I glorify myself, my glory is nothing;
itawhi abi damSabbax li haw damrin atton dalahan-u.
it is my Father who glorifies me, he of whom you say:He is our God.
wla ida'tonaihi: ana den yada'-na leh.
And you do not know him, but I do know him.
win amar-na dla yada'-na leh hawe-na li kaddaba akwatkon
If I said I do not know him, I would be a liar like you,

ella yada'-na leh wmilltah naTar-na.
but I do know him and keep his word.
abraham abukon msawax wa dyexze yawmi
Abraham, your father, rejoiced that he would see my day,
waxaza waxadi.
he saw it and was glad.
amen amen amar-na lkon
Truly, truly I tell to you,
d'adla ihwe abraham ana itai.
before Abraham was, I am.

Healing of the man born blind
                                                    J9,1-41
[His disciples asked: 'Who sinned that he was born blind?']
la hu xaTa wla abahawi
Neither he sinned nor his parents,
ella dtixzon beh 'abadawhi dalaha.
but that the works of God be made visible through him.
li wale lme'bbad 'abade dman dSaddrani 'ad imama-w:
I must work the works of him who sent me while it is day;
ate lilya dnaS la miSkax lmiplax.
night is coming when no one can work.
kma dab'alma-na nuhreh-na d'alma.
As long as I am in the world, I am the light of the world.

[To the blind man]
zel aSSig bma'amorita dSiloxa!
Go, wash in the pool of Siloam!
att mhaimin att babreh dnaSa?
Do you believe in the Son of man?
xazaitaihi whaw dammallel 'ammak huyu.
You have seen him and the one speaking with you is he.
[To the Pharisees]
ldineh d'alma hana etteit
For judgment I came into this world,
dailen dla xazein yexzon:
so that those who do not see may see,
waylen dxazein ismon.
and those who do see may become blind.
illu smaiya waiton lait wa lkon xaTaya.
If you were blind, you would not have sin.
haSa den amrin-tton: dxazein-nan
But now that you say: 'We see,'
miTTol hana xaTitkon qaiyama-y:
therefore your sin remains.

93

The Good Shepherd

J10, 1-18

amen amen amar-na lkon
Truly, truly, I tell you,

dman dla 'a'el min tar'a laTyara d'ana
anyone who does not enter the sheepfold by the gate

ella saleq min dukka xrenya haw gannaba-w wgaiyasa:
but climbs in by another way is a thief and a robber.

haw den d'a'el min tar'a ra'ya-w d'ana.
But the one who enters by the gate is the shepherd of the sheep.

walhana naTar tar'a patax leh tar'a
To him the gatekeeper opens the gate

w'ana Sam'a qaleh
and the sheep hear his voice

w'irbawhi qare baSmahaihon wmappeq lkon.
and he calls his sheep by their name and leads them out.

wma dappeq 'aneh qdameh azel
When he has led out his sheep, he walks ahead of them,

w'irbawhi dileh azin batreh miTTol dyad'in qaleh.
and his sheep follow him because they know his voice.

batar nukraya den la aza 'ana ella 'arqa minneh
The sheep will not follow a stranger, but they will flee from him,

dla yad'a qaleh dnukraya.
because they do not know the voice of a stranger.

amen amen amar-na lkon dana-na tar'a d'ana.
Truly, truly I tell you: I am the gate of the sheep.

wkullhon ailen dettau gannabe innon wgaiyase.
All who have come are thieves and robbers.

ella la Sim'at innon 'ana.
but the sheep did not listen to them.

dana-na tar'a.
I am the gate.

wbi in naS ye'ol ixxe:
Whoever enters by me will be saved,

wye'ol wippoq wre'ya iSkax.
and will come in and go out and find pasture.

gannaba la ate ella dignob wadiqTol wadyawbbed:
The thief comes only to steal and kill and destroy,

ana etteit dxaiye ihwon lhon wmiddem dyattir ihwe lhon.
I came that they may have life and have it more abundantly.

ana-na ra'ya Taba.
I am the good shepherd.

ra'ya Taba napSeh sa'em xalap 'aneh.
The good shepherd lays down his life for the sheep.

agira den dla hawa ra'ya wlau dileh innon 'irbe
The hired hand who is not shepherd and does not own the sheep,

95

ma daxza deba date Sabeq 'ana w'areq:
when he sees the wolf coming, leaves the sheep and flees;
wate deba xatep wambaddar lah l'ana.
and the wolf comes, snatches them and scatters the sheep.
agira den 'areq miTTol agira-w
A hireling flees, for he is a hireling
wla baTil leh 'al 'ana.
and does not care for the sheep.
ana-na ra'ya Taba: wyada'-na ldili wmitid'a-na min dili.
I am the good shepherd, I know my own and my own know me.
aikanna dyada' li abi wana yada'-na labi
As my Father knows me and I know my Father,
wnapSi sa'em-na xalap 'ana.
and I lay down my life for the sheep.
it li den ap 'irbe xrane ailen dla wau min Tyara hana:
And I have other sheep that are not of this fold;
wap lhon wale li lmaittayu innon wiSm'un qali.
I must bring them also and they will hear my voice.
wtihwe 'ana kullah xada wxad ra'ya.
So there will be one flock and one shepherd.
miTTol hana abi raxem li dana sa'em-na napSi
For this reason my Father loves me, because I lay down my life,
dtub esbih.
that I may take it up again.
la wa naS Saqel lah menni ella ana sa'em-na lah min cibyani.
No one takes it from me, but I lay it down of my own accord.
SalliT-na ger d'esimih wSalliT-na dtub esbih:
I have power to lay it down, and I have power to take it up again.
dhana puqdana qabblet min abi.
This command I have received from my Father.

At the festival of Dedication: I and my Father are one
J10,25-39

emret lkon wla mhaimnin-tton.
I have told you and you do not believe.
wa'abade dana 'abed-na baSmeh dabi hinnon sahdin 'alai:
The works that I do in my Father's name, they testify to me;
ella atton la mhaimnin-tton miTTol dla hawaiton min 'irbai.
aikanna demret lkon:
As I said to you:
'irbe dili qali Sam'in wana yada'-na lhon whinnon atein batari:
My sheep hear my voice, and I know them and they follow me;
wana yaheb-na lhon xaiye dal'alam wla yebdun l'alam:
and I give them eternal life, and they will never perish,

96

wla naS yexTop innon min idai.
and no one will snatch them out of my hand.
abi ger dyab li min koll rab-u
My Father who has given them to me is greater than all
wla naS miSkax dmin ideh dabi yexTop:
and no one can snatch them out of my Father's hand.
ana wabi xad xanan:
I and my Father we are one.
saggiye 'abade Sappire min lwat abi xawwitkon:
Many good works from my Father I have shown you,
miTTol aina 'abada minnhon ragmin-tton li?
for which work of these are you going to stone me?
la wa hakanna ktib bnamoskon: dana emret dalahe atton?
Is it not written in your law: 'I said, you are gods?'
in lhanon emar alahe miTTol dalwathon hawat millta dalaha
If he called them gods because to them came the word of God,
wla miSkax ktaba diStre: laina daba qaddSeh
and scripture cannot be broken: of him whom the Father sanctified
wSaddreh l'alma atton amrin-tton: damgaddep att:
and sent into the world do you say: 'You are blaspheming,'
'al demret Ikon: dabreh-na dalaha?
because I said: 'I am the Son of God?'
in la 'abed-na 'abade dabi la thaimnuni:
If I am not doing the works of my Father, then do not believe me.
in den abed-na apin li la mhaimnin-tton
But if I do them, even though you do not believe me,
lhon la'bade haimenu dtid'un
do believe the works, so that you may know
wathaimnun dabi bi wana babi.
and believe that my Father is in me and I am in my Father.

The mission of the Seventy

L 10,2-12 Mt10,7

xacada saggi wpa'ale z'orin:
The harvest is plentiful, but the workers are few,
b'au hakel min mare xacada
ask therefore the Lord of the harvest
dyappeq pa'ale laxacadeh.
to send out the workers into his harvest.
zelu ha ana mSaddar-na Ikon ak imre bainai debe:
Go! See, I am sending you like lambs among wolves.
la tiSqlun Ikon kise wla tarmale wla msane:
Carry no purses, no bags, no sandals:
wbaSlama dnaS burxa la tiSilun:
and greet no one on the way.

wlaina baita d'a'ellin-tton luqdam emaru:
Whatever house you enter, first say:
Slama lbaita hana!
'Peace to this house!'
win it tamman bar Slama
If son of peace is there,
ittnix 'alawhi Slamkon:
your peace will rest on him;
win den la Slamkon 'alaihon ihippoq.
but if not, your peace will return to you.
beh den bbaita hawau
Stay in that house,
kad la'asin-tton wSatein min dilhon:
eating and drinking from what they have,
Sawe-u ger pa'ala agreh.
for the worker is worthy of his wages.
wla tSannon min baita lbaita.
Do not move about from house to house.
wlaida mditta d'allin-tton wamqabblin lkon
Whatever town you enter and they welcome you,
l'asu middem dmittsim lkon.
eat what is set before you.
wassau lailen dakrihin bah wemaru:
And cure those who are sick in it, and say:
qirbbat 'alaikon malkuteh dalaha.
'The kingdom of God has come near to you.'
laida den mditta d'allin-tton
But whatever town you enter
wla iqabblunakon
and they do not welcome you,
poqu lkon bSuqa wemaru:
go out into its streets and say:
wap xella dadbeq lan briglain min mdittkon
'Even the dust clinging to our feet from your town
napcin-nan lkon.
we wipe off to you.
bram hade da'u
Yet know this:
dqirbbat 'alaikon malkuteh dalaha.
The kingdom of God has come near upon you.'
amar-na lkon dlasdom ihwe nix
I tell you that for Sodom it will be easier
byawma haw aw lamditteh hai:
on that day than for that city.

Woes to unrepentant towns

L 10,13-16

wai leki kurzin! wai leki bet caida!
Woe to you, Chorazin! Woe to you, Bethsaida!
dillu bcor wabcaidan hawau xaile dahawau bkein
For if in Tyre and Sidon the miracles had been done as in you,
kbar den bsaqqe wabqiTma tabu.
doubtless in sackcloth and ashes they would have repented.
bram lcor walcaidan ihwe nix
But for Tyre and Sidon will be easier
byawma ddina aw lkon.
in the day of judgment than for you.
watti kpar naxom hay da'adamma laSmaiya ittrimti?
And you, Capernaum, will you be exalted to heaven?
'adamma laSyol tittaxten!
You will be brought down to Hades!
man dalkon Sama' li Sama' wman dalkon Talem
Whoever listens to you listens to me, and whoever rejects you
li-u Talem: wman dli Talem Talem lman dSalxani:
rejects me, and whoever rejects me rejects the one who sent me.

The return of the Seventy

L 10,17-20

xaze weit leh lsaTana danpal ak barqa min Smaiya.
I watched Satan fall like lightning from heaven.
ha yaheb-na lkon SulTana dahwaiton daiSin xawawata
See, I have given you authority to tread on snakes
wa'aqarbe wkulleh xaileh dab'eldbaba:
and scorpions, and over all the power of the enemy;
wmiddem la yaharkon.
and nothing will hurt you.
bram bhade la tixdon dSede miSta'bbdin lkon
But do not rejoice in this that the spirits submit to you,
ella xadau daSmahaikon itktebu baSmaiya.
bur rejoice that your names are written in heaven.

The greatest commandment

L 10,25-28 Mt22,34 M12,29

boraita aikanna ktib?
What is written in the law?
aikanna qare att?
What do you read there?
Sma' israyel! marya alahan marya xad-u.
Hear, o Israel! The Lord our God the Lord is One.

99

wadtirxam lmarya alahak min kulleh libbak
and you shall love the Lord your God with all your heart
wmin kullah napSah wmin kulleh re'yanak
and with all your soul and with all your mind
wmin kulleh xailak:
and with all your strength.
hanaw puqdana rabba wqadmaya:
This is the greatest and first commandment.
wdatrein ddame leh: dtirxam lqarribak ak napSak:
And a second is like it: You shall love your neighbor as yourself.
bhalen trein puqdanin talya oraita wanbiyye:
On these two commandments hang all the law and the prophets.
la hawait raxxiq min malkuta dalaha:
You are not far from the kingdom of God.
trica'it emart: hade 'abed wtixxe:
You have answered right: do this and you will live.

The parable of Good Samaritan
L 10,29-37
gabra xad naxet wa min oriSlem lirixo
A man was going down from Jerusalem to Jericho
wanpalu 'alawhi lisTaye wSalxuhi wamxauhi
and robbers fell upon him and they stripped him, beat him
wSabquhi kad qallil qaiyama beh napSeh wezalu.
and left him while barely alive and went away.
wagdaS kahana xad naxet wa burxa hai.
And it so happened that a priest was going down that road.
waxazaihi wa'bar.
And when he saw him, he passed by.
whakanna ap lewya etta mTa lhai dukkta:
So likewise a Levite came to that place.
waxazaihi wa'bar.
And he saw him and passed by.
naS den Samraya kad rade wa etta aika ditawhi wa
But a Samaritan man while traveling came where he was,
waxazaihi witraxxam 'alawhi.
and he saw him and had pity for him.
witqarab wa'acab maxwateh
he came near to him and bandaged his wounds,
wancal 'alaihen xamra wmiSxa.
and poured over them wine and oil.
wsameh 'al xamareh waittyeh lputqa
Then he put him on his donkey and brought him to an inn
witbTel leh 'alawhi.
and took care of him.

100

walcapreh dyawma appeq trein deinarin:
And in the morning of the day he took out two denarii,
yab lputqaya wemar leh:
gave them to the innkeeper and said to him:
icap dileh win middem yattir tappeq
Take care of him and whatever more you spend,
dhapek-na yaheb-na lak.
when I come back, I will repay you.
mana hakel min halen tlata mitixze lak dahawa qarriba
Which of these three, do you think, was a neighbor
lhaw danpal bidai gaiyase?
to him who fell into the hands of the robbers?
zel ap att hakanna hawait 'abed.
Go you too and do likewise.

Martha and Mary
L 10,38-42
marta marta yacpatti warhibatti 'al saggiyata.
Martha, Martha, you are anxious and worried about many things.
xada-y den dmitba'ya: maryam den manta Tabta gbat lah
but only one thing is necessary, Mary has chosen the better part
hay dla titnseb minnah.
which will not be taken away from her.

Friend at midnight
L 11,5-8
mannu minnkon dit leh raxma wyezal lwateh
Which of you who has a friend and will go to him
bpelgut lilya wyemar leh: raxmi aSelaini tlat grican
at midnight and say to him: 'Friend, lend me three loaves,
miTTol draxma etta lwati min urxa
for a friend has arrived at my house from a journey,
wlait li middem dessim leh.
and I have nothing to set before him.'
whaw raxmeh min lgaww ye'ne wyemar leh:
and that friend of his from within will answer saying:
la taharani dha tar'a axid-u wabnai
'Do not bother me, the door is now shut and my children
'ammi b'arsa la miSkax-na dequm wetten lak?
are with me in bed, I cannot get up and give you anything?'
amar-na lkon din miTTol raxmuta la itten leh
I tell you, even though because of friendship he will not give him,
miTTol xacciputeh iqum winten leh kma dmatb'e leh.
because of his persistence he will get up and give him whatever
he needs.

101

True blessedness

L 11,28

Tubaihon lailen dSam'in millteh dalaha wnaTrin lah.
Blessed are rather those who hear the word of God and obey it.

A greedy man

L 12,14

gabra mannu aqqimani 'alaikon daiyana wampalgana?
Man, who set me a judge or arbitrator over you?

The parable of the rich fool

L 12,16-21

gabra xad 'attire a'alat leh ar'eh 'allata saggiyata
There was a rich man whose land produced a great harvest,
wmitxaSSab wa bnapSeh wamar:
and he thought to himself and said:
mana e'bed dlait li aika dexmol 'allati?
'What will I do, for I have nowhere to store my crops?'
wemar: hade e'bbed: estur beit qpasai
And he said: 'I will do this - I will tear down my barns
webne w'awreb innon.
and build larger ones.
wexmol tamman kulleh 'aburi wTabati wemar InapSi:
There I shall store all my grain and my goods and say to my soul:
napSi it leki Tabata saggiyata dsiman laSnaya saggiyata
My soul, you have many goods laid up for many years,
itnixi wakoli iStai itbassami.
rest, eat, drink, be merry.'
amar leh den alaha:
But God said to him:
xassir re'yana! bhana lilya napSak tab'in
'You fool! This night your life will be demanded
lah minnak whalen dTaiyebt lma ihwon?
from you, and the things you have prepared, whose will they be?'
hakanna-w man dsa'em leh simata wbalaha la 'attir.
So it is he who lays treasure for himself and is not rich in God.

Dependence on God

L 12,22-32

miTTol hana lkon amar-na: la tecppun lnapSkon
Therefore I tell you, do not worry about your life,
mana teklun wla lpagrkon mana tilbSun.
what you will eat or about your body , what you will wear.
napSa ger yattira min saibarta wpagra min lbuSa.
For life is more than food and the body more than clothing.

103

itbaqqau bna'abe dla zar'in wla xacdin
Consider the ravens: they neither sow nor reap,
wlait lhon tawwane wbeit qpase
and they have neither storerooms nor barns,
walaha mtarse lhon.
and yet God feeds them.
kma hakel atton yattirin-tton min parxata!
How much more valuable you are than the birds!
aina den minnkon kad yacep miSkax
And which of you by being anxious can
lmawsapu 'al qawmteh amta xada?
add a cubit to his stature?
in den apla z'orta miSkxin-tton
If the you cannot do even very little thing,
mana 'al Sarka yacpin-tton?
why do you worry about the rest?
itbaqqau bSoSanne aikanna rabyan wla layan wla 'azlan
Consider the lilies, how they grow, they do not toil or spin,
amar-na lkon den dap la Sleimon bkulleh Subxeh
but I tell you, not even Solomon in all his glory
itkassi ak xada min halen.
was clothed like one of them.
in den la'amira dyawmana itawhi bxaqla
if then the grass which is today in the field
wamxar napel btannura alaha hakanna malbeS
and tomorrow is cast into the oven God so clothes,
kma yattir lkon z'orai haimanuta?
how much more you, you of little faith?
watton la tib'on mana teklun wmana tiSton
You do not seek what you are to eat and what you are to drink,
wla yephe re'yankon bhalen.
and do not be of anxious mind about that.
halen ger kullhen amme-w d'alma ba'ein.
For these things all the nations of the world seek.
ap lkon den abukon yada' dmitba'yan lkon halen.
and your Father knows that you need these things.
bram ba'u malkuteh dalaha
But seek the kingdom of God,
whalen kullhen mittawspan lkon.
and these things will be added to you.
la tidxal gzara z'ora dacba abukon
Fear not, little flock, for your Father chose
ditten lkon malkuta:
to give you the kingdom.

Treasures in heaven

L 12,33-34

zabbenu qinyankon whabu zidqeta.
Sell your possessions and give alms.

'abedu lkon kise dla balein
Make purses for yourselves that do not wear out,

wsimta dla gaiza baSmaiya
and an unfailing treasure in heaven,

aika dgannaba la qareb wsasa mxabbel.
where no thief comes near nor moth destroys.

aika ger diteh simatkon tamman ihwe ap libbkon.
For where your treasure is, there will be also your heart.

The parable of vigilant servants

L 12,35-48

ihwon assirin xaccaikon wmanharin Sragaikon
Let your loins be girded and have your lamps lit,

wahwau damein lnaSa damsakkein lmarhon
and be like men who are waiting for their master

demmati ipne min beit miStuta
when he returns from the wedding banquet,

dma etta wanqaS mixda iptxun leh.
so as soon as he comes and knocks they may open to him.

Tubaihon l'abde hanon ailen dyete marhon
Blessed are those servants whom when their master comes

wiSkax innon kad 'irin.
finds them vigilant.

amen amar-na lkon: dyesor xaccawhi wismek innon
Truly, I tell you, he will fasten his belt and have them sit down to eat

wye'bbar iSammeS innon.
and he will come around and serve them.

win bmaTTarta dtartein aw dtlat yete
And if he comes in the second or third watch

yiSkax hakanna Tubaihon l'abde hanon.
and finds them so, blessed are those servants.

hade den da'u: dillu yada' wa mare baita
But know this: if the owner of the house had known

baida maTTarta ate gannaba mitt'ir wa
at what hour the thief was coming, he would have watched

wla Sabeq wa dittippleS baiteh.
and not let his house to be broken into.

ap atton hakel hawau mTaiyabe
You also must be ready,

dbhai Sa'ta dla sabrin-tton ate breh dnaSa.
for at the hour you do not expect the Son of man will come.

L 12,42-48

mannu kai itawhi rabb baita mhaimna xakkima
Who then is the faithful and prudent manager
daiqimiwhi mareh 'al tiSmiSteh
whom his master will put in charge of his servants
dintan prasa bzabneh?
to give them their allowance at the proper time?
Tubawhi lhaw 'abda dyete mareh
Blessed is that servant whom his master when he comes
iSxiwhi d'abed hakanna.
finds him doing so.
Sarrira'it amar-na lkon daiqimiwhi 'al kulleh qinyaneh.
Truly I tell you, he will put him in charge of all his possessions.
in den yemar 'abda haw blibbeh: dmari mawxar lmeta
But if that servant says in his heart: My master is late in coming
waiSarre lmimxa l'abde wlamhata dmareh
and begins to beat the menservants and maids of his master,
waiSarre lmel'as walmiSta walmirwa.
and begins to eat and drink and get drunk.
yete mareh d'abda haw byawma dla sabar
The master of that servant will come on a day he does not expect
wabSa'ta dla yada' wipilgiwhi
and at an hour he does not know, and will punish him,
waisim mnateh 'am hanon dla mhaimnin.
and assign him a place with the unbelievers.
'abda den aina dyada' cibyana dmareh
That servant who knew his master's will,
wla Taiyeb leh ak cibyaneh nibla' saggiyata
but did not get ready as was his will, will be beaten a lot.
haw den dla yada'
But the one who did not know
w'abed middem dSawe lmaxwata
and did what deserved a beating,
ibla maxwata z'oriyata.
will receive a light beating.
koll ger ditiheb leh saggi:
Everyone to whom much is given,
saggi ittba' minneh.
much will be required of him.
wlhaw ditge'el leh saggi
and to whom is entrusted much,
yattira'it itbbe'un bideh.
more will be demanded of him.

Division in the family
L 12,49-53

nura atteit darme bar'a wcabe-na illu min kaddu xebbat!
I came to cast fire upon the earth and wish it were already lit!

wma'modita it li de'mad
I have a baptism with which to be baptized,

wsaggi allic-na 'adamma dtiStamle.
and I am greatly distressed until it is completed!

sabrin-tton dSaina etteit darme bar'a?
Do you think that I came to bring peace on earth?

amar-na Ikon: dla ella palgwata.
I tell you: No, but rather division.

min haSa ger ihwon xammSa bbaita xad dapligin:
From now on five in one household will be divided:

tlata 'al trein wtrein 'al tlata.
three against two and two against three.

itpleg ger aba 'al breh
They will be divided: father against his son,

wabra 'al abuhi immam 'al bartah
and son against his father, mother against her daughter

wbarta 'al immah xamata 'al kalltah
and daughter against her mother, mother-in-law against her

wkallta 'al xamatah.
daughter-in-law and daughter-in-law against her mother-in-law.

A call to repentance
L 13,1-5

sabrin-tton dhanon glilaye xaTTayin wau yattir
Do you think that these Galileans were worse sinners

min kullhon glilaye dhakanna hawa innon ?
than all the other Galileans, because they suffered this way?

la: amar-na Ikon den dap kullhon in la ttubun
No, I tell you, but unless you repent,

hakanna tebdun.
you will all likewise perish.

aw hanon tmanta'sar danpal 'alaihon magdla bSiloxa
Or those eighteen upon whom the tower of Siloam fell

wqaTTel innon: sabrin-tton dxaTTayin wau yattir
and killed them, do you think that they were worse sinners

min kullhon bnainaSa d'amrin boriSlem?
than all the men who live in Jerusalem?

la: amar-na Ikon din la ttubun kullhon
No, I tell you, but if you do not repent,

akwathon tebdun.
you will likewise perish.

107

The parable of the barren fig tree

L 13,6-9

tetta it wat InaS danciba bkarmeh
A man had a fig tree planted in his vineyard,
wetta b'a bah pere wla iSkax.
and he came looking for fruit on it but found none.
wemar Ipallaxa: ha tlat Snin ate-na
And he said to the gardener: 'See, for three years I have come
ba'e pere btetta hade wla miSkax-na:
looking for fruit on this fig tree but have found none.
psoqeh! Imana mbaTla ar'a?
Cut it down! Why should it be wasting the soil?'
amar leh pallaxa: mari Sboqeh ap hade Satta
The gardener said to him: 'Sir, leave it for this year also,
'ad epelxih wezablih win 'abdat pere:
until I dig around it and fertilize it, maybe it will bear fruit;
win la Imanxai tipsqih.
if not, next year you can cut it down.'

The healing of the crippled woman

L 13,12-16

attta Saryatti min kurhaneki!
Woman, you are set free from your ailment!
naseb bappe! xad xad minnhon bSabbta la Sare tawreh
You hypocrites! Does not each of you on the Sabbath untie his ox
aw xamareh min orya wazel maSqe?
or his donkey from the manger and lead it out for watering?
hade den dbarteh hi dabraham wasreh akelqarca
And this daughter of Abraham, whom Satan bound
ha tmana'esre Snin la wale wa dtiSre
now for eighteen years, should she not be set free
min hana assurya byawma dSabbta?
from this bondage on the Sabbath day?

The narrow door

L 13,24-30

itkattaSu Ime"al btar'a allica:
Strive to enter by the narrow door,
amar-na Ikon ger dsaggiye ib'on Ime"al wla iSkxun.
I tell you, for many will try to enter and will not be able.
min Sa'ta daiqum mare baita wyexod tar'a
Once the owner of the house gets up and shuts the door
wtihwon qaimin Ibar wnaqSin btar'a
you will stand outside knocking on the door

watSarron lmemar: maran ptax lan!
and begin saying: Lord, open to us!
wye'ne hu wyemar:
And he will reply and will say:
dla yada'-na aimikka atton.
I do not know where you are from.
watSarron lmemar: qdamaik ekkaln wiStin
Then you will begin to say: We ate and drank with you
wabSuqain allept.
and in our streets you taught.
wyemar lkon: la yada'-na aimikka atton
But he will say: I do not know where you are from,
proqu atton menni palxai Suqra!
go away from me, all you evildoers!
tamman ihwe bikya wxuraq Sinne:
There will be weeping and gnashing of teeth,
kad texzon labraham wlisxaq walyaq'ob
when you see Abraham and Isaac and Jacob
wakullhon nbiyye bmalkuta daSmaiya
and all the prophets in the kingdom of heaven,
atton ger tihwon mappqin lbar.
but you yourselves thrown out.
wyeton min madinxa wmin ma'arba wmin taimna
And people will come from east and west, from north
wmin garbya wistamkun bmalkuta dalaha.
and south, and sit at the table in the kingdom of God.
wha it xraye dihwon qadmaye
And behold, some are last who will be first,
wit qadmaye dihwon xraye.
and some are first who will be last.

About Herod
L 13,31-33

zelu emmaru lta'la hana:
Go and tell that fox:
dha mappeq-na Sede waswata 'abed-na
Behold, I cast out demons and make cures
yawmana wamxar walyawma datlata miStamle-na.
today and tomorrow and on third day I finish my work.
bram wale li dyawmana wamxar es'or
Yet I must work today and tomorrow
walyawma xrana ezal
and next day be on my way,
miTTol dla miSkxa danbiyya yebad lbar min oriSlem.
for it is impossible for a prophet to die outside of Jerusalem.

The lament over Jerusalem

oriSlem oriSlem qaTlat nbiyye
O Jerusalem, Jerusalem, you who kill the prophets
wragmat lailen daSlixin lwatah!
and stone those who are sent to you!
kma zabnin cbet lamknaSu bnaiki
How many times I desired to gather your children together
ak tarnagulta dkanSa parugeh txet gippeh wla cbaiton!
as a hen gathers her chicks under her wings and you would not!
ha miStbeq Ikon baitkon xarba.
See, your house is left to you desolate.
amar-na Ikon ger dla texzonani 'adamma dtemrun:
And I tell you, you will not see me until you say:
brik-u date baSmeh dmarya.
'Blessed is the one who comes in the name of the Lord.'

The man with dropsy

L14,1-6

din SalliT bSabbta lmassayu?
Is it lawful to cure on the Sabbath?
mana minnkon dippel breh aw tawreh bbera
Who among you if a son or an ox that has fallen into a well
byawma dSabbta wla mixda dla masseq leh?
on a Sabbath day will not immediately pull him out?

The parable of the guests

L14,7-14

emmati dmizdamman att min naS lbeit miStuta
When you are invited by someone to a wedding banquet,
la tezal tistmek lak breS smaka
do not go and sit down at the head of the table,
dalma ihwe mzamman tamman naS damyaqqar minnak
for may be someone have been invited there greater than you
wyete haw man dlak wleh qra wemar lak:
and he who invited you both may come and say to you:
dhab dukkta lhana: wtibhat kad qa'em att
'Give place to this man.' And then with shame you will get up
waxed att dukkta xraita.
and take the lowest place.
ella ma dizdammant zel istamak lak bxarta
But when you are invited, go and sit in the back,
dma detta haw daqrak yemar lak:
so that when the host comes he may say to you:

111

raxemi it'alla l'el wistmek! wtihwe lak tiSboxta
'My friend, move up higher!' Then you will have honor
qdam kullhon dasmikin 'ammak.
before all who are sitting at table with you.
miTTol dkoll dairim napSeh itmakkak:
For everyone who exalts himself will be humbled,
wkoll dyammek napSeh ittrim.
and he who humbles himself will be exalted.
ma d'abed att Saruta aw xaSamita la tihwe qare
When you give a dinner or a banquet, do not invite
raxmaik apla axaik aw xyanaik wla Sbabaik 'attire
your friends and brothers or relatives and rich neighbors,
dalma ap hinnon iqronak wihwe lak pur'ana hana.
in case they might invite you back and you would be repaid.
ella ma d'abed att qubbala qri lmiskene sgipe xagise
But when you give a banquet, invite the poor, the crippled, the lame
smaiya: wTubaik dlait lhon dipr'unak.
the blind and you are blessed, because the cannot repay you.
ihwe ger pur'anak baqyama dzaddiqe.
For you will be repaid at the resurrection of the just.

The parable of the great dinner
L 14,16-24
gabra xad 'abad xaSamita rabbta waqra Isaggiye
A man gave a great dinner and invited many
wSaddar 'abdeh b'idanna daxSamita dyemar
and sent his servant at the time for the dinner to say
lailen daqrein: ha koll middem mTaiyab lkon tau:
to those invited: Now everything is ready for you, come!
wSarriyu min xad kullhon lmiStalu.
But they began all alike to make excuses.
amar leh qadmaya: qrita zibnet wallic-na deppoq exzeh:
The first said to him: I bought a field, and I must go out to see it,
ba'e-na minnak Sboqaini dmiStel-na.
I beg you allow me to be excused.
xrena amar: xammSa zawggin tawre zibnet wazel-na
Another said: I bought five yoke of oxen and I am going
debqe innon: ba'e-na minnak Sboqaini dmiStel-na.
to try them out, I beg you allow me to be excused.
xrena amar: attta nisbet miTTol hade la miSkax-na dete.
Another said: I married a woman and therefore I cannot come.
wetta haw 'abda wemar lmareh halen.
And the servant came and told to his master these things.
haiden rgez mare baita wemar l'abdeh:
Then the owner of the house got angry and said to his servant:

112

poq ba'agal lSuqe walberyata damditta
Go out at once into the streets and lanes of the city
wa'el lka lmiskene walmak'abe wlamxagre wla'awire.
and bring here the poor, the cripples, the blind and the lame.
wemar 'abda: mari wa ak dapqaddet wtub it atra.
The servant said: Sir, it is done as you ordered and still there is room.
wemar mara l'abdeh: poq lurxata
And the master said to his servant: Go out into the roads
walbeit syage walloc dye'lun
and hedgerows and compel them to come in,
ditmle baiti.
so that my house may be filled.
amar-na lkon ger dxad min hanon naSa daqrein wau
For I tell you, none of those who were invited
la iT'amun min xaSamiti.
will taste of my dinner.

Discipleship
                                    L 14,25-27 M10,37-38

man date lwati wla sane labuhi wlimmeh
Whoever comes to me and does not hate his father and mother,
wlaxawhi wlaxwateh wlattteh wlabnawhi wap lnapSeh
brothers and sisters, his wife and children, even his own life,
talmida la miSkax dihwe li.
cannot be my disciple.
wman dla Saqel clibeh wate batari
Whoever does not carry his cross and come after me
talmida la miSkax dihwe li.
cannot be my disciple.

The parables of a tower and an army
                                    L 14,28-33
mannu ger minnkon dcabe dibne magdla
For which of you wishing to build a tower,
wla luqdam yateb xaSeb napqateh
does not first sit down and estimate the cost
in it leh lamSallamuteh?
if he has enough to complete it?
dla kad isim Satasta wla iSkax lamSallamu
Otherwise, when he has laid a foundation and is not able to finish
koll dxazein ihwon mbazzxin beh wamrin:
all who see it will laughing at him and saying:
dhana gabra Sarri lmibna wla iSkax lamSallamu.
'This fellow began to build and was not able to finish.'

mannu malka dazel laqraba lmitkattaSu 'am malka xabreh
What king going out to wage war with a neighboring king,
wla luqdam mitra'e din miSkax b'esra alpin
will not first consider if he is able with ten thousand
lmera' lhaw date 'alawhi b'esrin alpin?
to meet him who comes against him with twenty thousand?
win den la 'ad hu raxxiq minneh
And if not, while the other is still far away from him,
mSaddar izdagge wba'e 'al Slama.
he sends envoys and asks for peace.
hakanna koll naS minnkon dla Sabeq kulleh qinyaneh
So then, whoever of you does not leave all his possessions
la miSkax dihwe li talmida.
he cannot be my disciple.

The parable of salt

L 14,34   M9,49   Mt5,13

koll ger bnura mitimlax.
For everyone will be salted with fire.
atton innon milxah dar'a.
You are the salt of the earth.
Sappira-y milxa: in den ap milxa tipkah bmana titemlax?
Salt is good but if salt goes flat, with what will it be salted?
la lar'a wla lzibla azla lbar Sadein lah.
It is fit neither for the soil nor the manure pile, it is thrown out.
man dit leh idne diSma' iSma'.
He who has ears to hear, let him hear.

The parable of the lost coin

L 15,8-10

aw aida-y attta dit lah 'esra zuzin wtawbed xad minnhon
Or what woman, if she has ten silver coins and loses one of them,
wla manhara Sraga wxama baita wba'ya bTila'it
does not light a lamp and sweep the house and search carefully
'adamma dtiSkxiwhi?
until she finds it?
wma diSkaxateh qarya lraxmatah
When she has found it, she calls together her friends
wlaSbabatah wamra lahen:
and neighbors, saying to them:
xadaein 'ammi diSkxet zuzi dabbid wa.
Rejoice with me, for I have found my coin which I had lost.
amar-na lkon dhakanna tihwe xaduta qdam malakawhi
I tell you, just so there is joy before the angels
dalaha 'al xad xaTTaya dta'eb.
of God over one sinner who repents.

114

The parable of the prodigal son

L 15,11-32

lgabra xad it wa leh bnaiya trein wemar breh leh z'ora:
A man had two sons and the younger of them said to him:
abi hab li palguta dmajya li min baitak.
'Father, give me the share that is coming to me from your house.'
wpalleg lhon qinyaneh.
So he divided between them his property.
wmin batar yawmata qallil kanneS hu breh z'ora kollmiddem
A few days later the younger son gathered all whatever
damTaihi wezal latra raxxiqa.
he had and traveled to a distant country.
wtamman baddar qinyaneh kad xaiye parxa'it.
And there he squandered his property living lavishly.
wkad gammar koll middem dit wa leh
And when he had spent everything he had
hawa kapna rabba batra haw wSarri xasar leh.
a great famine arose in that country and he began to be in need.
wezal nqep leh lxad min bnai mditta datra haw
So he went and hired himself out to one of that country's citizens,
whaw Saddreh laqrita lmir'a xazire.
who sent him to his fields to feed the pigs.
wmitragrag wa lmimla karseh min xarrube hanon
And he craved to fill his stomach with the husks that
daklin waw xazire wla naS yaheb wa leh.
the pigs were eating, and no one gave him anything.
wkad etta lwat napSeh emar: kma haSa agire it
But when he came to himself he said: How many hired men now
beit abi dyattir lhon laxma wana harka lkapni abed-na.
in my father's house have more bread and here I perish of hunger.
equm ezal lwat abi wemar leh:
I will get up and go to my father and I will say to him:
abi xaTet baSmaiya waqdamaik wla mikkel Sawe-na
'Father, I sinned against heaven and you, I am no longer worthy
dabrak etiqre 'abedani ak min agirak.
to be called your son, make me as one of your hired men.'
wqam etta lwat abuhi.
So he got up and came to his father.
w'ad hu raxxiq xazaihi abuhi
But while he was still far off, his father saw him and
witraxxam 'alawhi warxeT npal 'al cawreh wnaSqeh.
had compassion for him, he ran, fell on his neck and kissed him.
wemar leh breh: abi xaTet baSmaiya waqdamaik
And the son said to him: 'Father, I sinned against heaven and you

115

wla mikkel Sawe-na dabrak etiqre.
and no longer I am worthy to be called your son.'
emar den abuhi l'abdawhi: appequ isTla reSaita
But the father said to his servants: 'Bring the best robe,
albSuhi wsimu 'izzaqta bideh wasanuhi msane
dress him and put a ring on his hand and put shoes on him,
waittau qTolu tawra dpiTma wnekol wnitbassam
bring out and kill the fatted calf and let us eat and celebrate,
dhana beri mita wa waxaiya wabbida wa wiStekax.
for this son of mine was dead and is alive, he was lost and is found.'
wSarriyu lmitbassamu.
And they began to celebrate.
haw den breh qaSSiSa baqrita wa wkad etta
Now the elder son was in the field and as he came
waqreb lwat baita Sma' qal zmara dsaggiye.
and neared the house, he heard the sound of singing of many.
waqra lxad min Tlaye wSaleh mana-w hana.
And he called one of the boys and asked what this was.
amar leh: axuk etta waqTal abuk
And he said to him: 'Your brother came and your father killed
tawra dpiTma dkad xalim aqbleh.
the fatted calf, because he got him back safe and sound.'
wargez wla cabe wa lme'al.
Then he became angry and refused to go in .
wanpaq abuhi b'a minneh:
His father came out and pleaded with him.
hu den emar abuhi:
But he said to his father:
ha kma Snin pallax-na lak 'abduta
'Look, all these years I have been working like a slave for you and
wla mtom 'ebret puqdanak wmin mtom gadya la yabt li
I never disobeyed your command, yet you never gave me a goat
ditbassam 'am raxmai.
that I might celebrate with my friends.
lhana den brak kad parax qinyanak
But when this son of yours wasted your wealth
'am zanyata wetta nkast leh tawra dpiTma?
with harlots and came, you slaughtered for him the fatted calf?'
amar leh abuhi: beri att bkollzban 'ammi att
His father said to him: 'My son, you are always with me
wkoll middem dili dilak-u.
and all that is mine is yours.
lmibsam den wale wa lan walmixda
But we had to celebrate and rejoice,
dhana axuk mita wa waxaiya wabbida wa wiStkax.
for this your brother was dead and is alive, was lost and is found.'

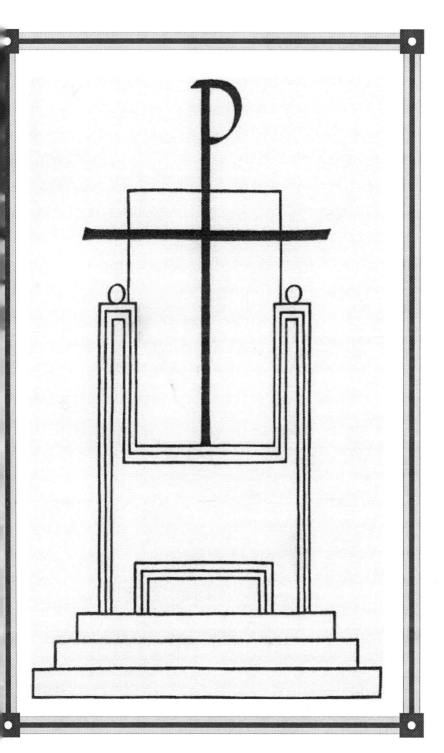

The parable of the unjust steward
L 16, 1-9

gabra xad it wa 'attire wit leh rabb baita
There was a rich man who had a steward
witakelu leh qarcawhi dqinyaneh mparax.
and they have accused him of squandering his property.
waqrawhi mareh wemar leh:
His master called him and said to him:
manaw hana dSama'-na 'alaik?
'What is that I hear about you?
hab li xuSbana drabbat baitutak.
Give me an accounting of your management,
la ger miSkax att mikkel rabb baita dtihwe li.
because you cannot be my steward any longer.'
amar haw rabb baita bnapSeh:
Then the steward said to himself:
mana 'ebbed dmari Saqel lah menni rabbat baituta?
What will I do, now that my master is taking the position from me?
dexpor la miSkax-na walmixdar baxet-na.
To dig I am unable and to beg I am ashamed.
yed'et mana e'bbed dma dnippqet min rabbat baituta
I know what I shall do so that when I am removed as manager,
iqabblunani bbattaihon.
they may welcome me into their homes.
waqra lxad xad min xaiyabe dmareh wemar lqadmaiya:
So calling one by one his master's debtors, he asked the first:
mana xaiyab att lmari?
'How much do you owe my master?'
amar leh: ma' mataryan miSxa.
He said: 'A hundred jugs of olive oil.'
amar leh: sab ktabak wteb ba'agal ktob xammSin mataryan.
He said to him: 'Take your bill, sit down quickly and write it fifty jugs.'
wemar laxrena: watt kma xaiyab att lmari?
Then he asked another: 'And how much do you owe my master?'
amar leh: ma' korin xiTTe.
he said: 'A hundred containers of wheat.'
amar leh: qabbel ktabak wteb ktob tmanin korin.
He said to him: 'Take your bill, sit down, write it eighty containers.'
wSabbax maran lrabb baita d'awla dxakkkima'it 'abad
The master praised the unjust steward, for he acted shrewdly;
bnawhi ger d'alma hana xakkimin innon min bnawhi dnuhara
for the sons of this world are more shrewd than the sons of light
bSarbathon hade.
in dealing with their own generation.

118

wap ana amar-na Ikon d'abedu Ikon raxme
And I tell you. make friends for yourselves
min mamona hana d'awla dma dagmar
by means of dishonest wealth so that when it is gone,
iqabblunakon bamTallahon dal'alam.
they may welcome you into their eternal homes.

Faithfulness

L 16,10-12

man dabqallil mhaiman ap bsaggi mhaiman-u
He who is faithful in a very little is also faithful in much,
wman dabqallil 'awwal ap bsaggi 'awwal-u.
and he who is dishonest in a very little is dishonest also in much.
in hakel bmamona d'awla mhaimne la hawaiton
If then you have not been faithful in the dishonest mammon,
Srara Ikon mannu mhaimen?
the true riches who will entrust to you?
win badla dilkon la iStkaxton mhaimne
And if you have not been faithful in what it belongs to another
dilkon mannu itten Ikon?
who will give you what is your own?

Justice before men — to the Pharisees

L 16,14

atton innon damzaddqin napShon qdam bnainaSa
You are those who justify yourselves before men,
alaha den yada' libbawatkon dmiddem dram beit bnainaSa
but God knows your hearts, for what is valued among men
qdam alaha ndid-u.
in God's sight is detestable.

The parable of the rich man and Lazarus

L 16,19-31

gabra den xad 'attire it wa wlabeS wa buca wargwana
There was a rich man who was dressed in purple and linen
wkollyom mitbassam wa gaya'it.
and every day he was feasting joyously.
wmiskena xad it wa daSmeh la'azar.
And there was a poor man whose name was Lazarus.
warme wa lwat tar'eh dhaw 'attira
And he was lying at the gate of that rich man,
kad msaxxai bSuxne: wmitya'ab wa dimle karseh
being afflicted with sores and longing to fill his stomach
min partute dnaplin min patureh dhaw 'attire.
with the crumbs that fell from the table of that rich man.

119

ella ap kalbe atein waw mlaxakin Suxnawhi.
But even the dogs would come and lick his sores.
hawa den wmit haw miskena
It happened that the poor man died
wawbluhi malake l'ubbeh dabraham.
and the angels carried him to the bosom of Abraham.
ap haw den 'attira mit witiqbar.
And also that rich man died and was buried.
wkad miSttannaq baSyol arim 'ainawhi min ruxqa
And while he was tormented in Hades, he lifted his eyes from afar
waxaza labraham walla'azar b'ubbeh.
and saw Abraham and Lazarus by his side.
waqra bqala rama wemar:
And he cried out in a loud voice saying:
abi abraham itraxam 'alai wSaddar lla'azar
'Father Abraham, have mercy on me, and send Lazarus
dicbo' reS cib'eh bmaiya wyarTeb li liSSani
to dip the tip of his finger in water and cool my tongue,
dha miStannaq-na bSalhebta hade.
for I am tormented in these flames.'
amar leh abraham: beri itdakir dqabbelt
Abraham said to him: 'My son, remember that you received
Tabatak bxaiyaik wla'azar biSateh
your good things during your life, and Lazarus his evil things;
whaSa ha mittnix harka watt miSttannaq.
but now he is comforted here, and you are tormented.
w'am halen kullhen hawta rabbta sima banyan walkon
And besides all this, a great chasm is set between us and you,
wailen dcabein mikka dye'brun lwatkon
so that those who wish to pass from here to you
la iSkxun wapla dmin tamman ye'brun lwatan.
cannot do so and no one can cross from there to us.'
emar leh: maden ba'e-na minnak abi datSaddriwhi
And he said: 'Then, father, I beg you to send him
lbeit abi xammSa ger axin it li yezal
to my father's house, for I have five brothers, that he may go
isahed innon dla ap innon yeton ldukkta hana dtaSniqa.
to warn them lest they too come to this place of torment.'
amar leh abraham:
Abraham said to him:
it lhon muSe wanbiyye: iSim'un innon.'
They have Moses and the prophets, let them listen to them.
hu den amar leh: la abi abraham:
But he said to him: 'No, father Abraham.

ella in naS min mite yezal lwathon taibin.
But if someone from the dead goes to them, they will repent.'
amar leh abraham:
Abraham said to him:
in lmuSe wlanbiyye la Sam'un
'If to Moses and the prophets they do not listen,
apla in naS min mite iqum mhaimnin leh.
even if someone rises from the dead they will not believe him.'

Warning against scandals

L17,1-3 Mt18,6-7

la miSkxa dla yeton mikSule:
It is impossible that scandals should not come:
wai den lhaw dbideh yeton.
but woe to him through whom they come.
paqqax wa leh illu raxya daxamara talya bcawreh
It would be better for him if a millstone were hung around his neck
waSde byamma aw dyakSel lxad min halen z'ore.
and thrown into the sea than to scandalize one of these little ones.

On forgiveness

L17,3-4 Mt18,15

izdaru bnapSkon! in ixTe axuk kei beh:
Be on your guard! If your brother sins, rebuke him;
win ta'eb Sboq leh.
and if he repents forgive him.
win Sba' zabnin byawma yaskel bak
And if he offends you seven times in a day,
waSba' zabnin byawma itipne lwatak wyemar:
and if seven times in a day he turns back to you and says:
dta'eb-na: Sboq leh.
'I repent,' forgive him.

On faith

L17,5-6 Mt17,19

in it wat lkon haimanuta ak pridta dxardla
if you had faith like a grain of mustard
amrin waiton ltuta hana:
you would say to this mulberry tree:
dit'aqir witnacibb byamma
'Be uprooted and planted in the sea,'
wmiStma' wa lkon.
and it would obey you.

Unworthy servants

L 17,7-10

mannu den minnkon dit leh 'abda ddabar paddana
Who among you, who has a servant plowing
aw dra'e 'ana win yete min xaqla
or tending sheep and if he comes from the field,
amar leh mixda:
would say to him right away:
'abar istamak.
'Come over and sit at the table.'
ella amar leh:
Would he not rather say to him:
Taiyeb li middem daxSem wassor xaccaik:
'Prepare for me to eat and put on your apron,
SammeSaini 'adamma del'as weSte
serve me while I eat and drink,
wbatarken ap att til'as wtiSte.
after that you may also eat and drink.'
Ima Taibuteh mqabbel dhaw 'abda d'abad middem
Will that servant receive thanks because he did the things
ditipqed leh? la sabar-na.
which were commanded him? I do not think so.
hakanna ap atton ma 'abadton kullhen
So you also, when you have done all
ailen dapqidan Ikon emmaru:
that is commanded you, say:
d'abde xnan baTTile
'We are unworthy servants,
dmiddem dxaiyabin wain Ime'bbad 'abaden.
because what we ought to do we have done.'

Ten lepers

L 17,11-19

zelu xawwau napSkon Ikahane!
Go! Show yourselves to the priests!
la wa 'esra hawein halen ditdakkiyu: aika innon tiS'a?
Were not ten those who were cleansed, where are the nine?
Ima praSu dyeton intun tiSboxtta lalaha
Was no one found to return and give praise to God
ella hana dmin 'amma-w nukraya?
except this one from the foreign people?
qum zel haimanutak axyatak!
Rise and go, your faith made you well.

122

On the coming of the kingdom of God

L 17,20-21

la atya malkuteh dalaha banTurata:
The kingdom of God is not coming by observation:
wla amrin: ha harka-y wha har tamman-y
nor will they say: 'Look, here it is!' or 'There it is!'
ha ger malkuteh dalaha lgaww minnkon-y.
For behold, the kingdom of God is within you.

The Day of the Son of Man

L 17,22-37

yeton yawmata dtitragregun lmexza xad min yawmata
The days will come when you will long to see one of the days
dabreh dnaSa wla texzon.
of the Son of man and you will not see it.
win yemrun lkon: ha harka-w wha har tamman-u la tezun!
If they will say to you: 'Look here! Look there!' Do not go off!
aikanna ger dbarqa bareq min Smaiya wkulleh txet Smaiya
For just as a lightning flashes from the sky and under the sky
manhar hakanna ihwe breh dnaSa byawmeh.
lights up, so will be the Son of man in his day.
luqdam den 'atid-u dyexaS saggiyata
But first he must suffer many things
wistle min Sarbta hade.
and be rejected by this generation.
waikanna dahawa byawmateh dnox
Just as it was in the days of Noah,
hakanna ihwe byawmateh dabreh dnaSa.
so too will be in the days of the Son of man.
daklin waw wSatein wnasbin niSSe wyabbin lgabre
They ate and drank, they married and were given in marriage,
'adamma lyawma d'al nox lkewella
until the day Noah entered the ark,
wetta Tawpana wawbed kollnaS.
and the flood came and destroyed all of them.
waikanna tub dahawa byawmateh dloT:
Likewise, as it was in the days of Lot:
daklin waw wSatein wzabnin wamzabbnin wnacbin wbanein
they ate and drank, they bought and sold, they planted and built,
byawma den danpaq loT min sdom amTar marya
but on that day that Lot left Sodom the Lord rained
nura wkebrita min Smaiya wawbed lkullhon.
fire and sulfur from heaven and destroyed all of them.
hakanna ihwe byawma dmitgle breh dnaSa.
So will be on the day when Son of man is revealed.

123

bhaw yawma min dbiggara-w wmanawhi bbaita
On that day anyone on the housetop whose goods are in the house
la ixxot dyaSqol innon
must not go down to get them,
wman dabxaqla-w la ithepek lbestreh.
and anyone in the field must not turn back.
itdakiru lattteh dloT.
Remember Lot's wife.
man dcabe dyaxe napSeh yawbdih:
Whoever seeks to save his life will lose it,
wman dyawbed napSeh yaxxeih.
and whoever loses his life will save it.
amar-na lkon dhaw lilya trein ihwon bxada 'arsa
I tell you, on that night there will be two in one bed
xad ittdbar waxrena iStbeq.
one will be taken and the other left.
wtarteyin ihiwyan Taxnan akda:
There will be two women grinding meal together,
xada tittdbar waxreta tiStbeq.
one will be taken and the other left.
aika dpagra tamman itkanSun niSre.
Where the corpse is, there the vultures will gather.

The parable of the unjust judge
L 18, 1-8
daiyana xad it wa bamditta xada dmin alaha la daxel wa
There was a judge in one town who neither feared God
wmin bnainaSa la mitkaxad wa.
nor had respect for people.
armalta den xada it wat bamditta hay
There was a widow in that town
watya wat lwateh wamra: tba'aini min b'elddini.
and she came to him saying: 'Defend me against my opponent.'
wla cabe wa zabna saggiya batarken den emar bnapSeh:
He refused for a long time, but later he said to himself:
in min alaha la daxel-na wmin bnainaSa la mitkaxad-na
Though I have no fear of God and no respect for people,
apin miTTol malaya li hade armalta
yet because this widow keeps bothering me,
itb'ih dla bkoll 'iddan tihwe atya mahara li.
I will defend her lest continually coming she wear me out.
Sma'u mana emar daiyana d'awla!
Listen to what the unjust judge says!
alaha den la yattira'it ye'bbed tba'ta lagbawhi
And will not God all the more grant justice to his elect,

124

dqarein leh bimama wablilya wmaggar ruxeh 'alaikon?
who call to him day and night and will he delay long over them?
amar-na lkon dye'bbed tba'thon ba'agal.
I tell you, he will grant justice to them quickly.
bram yete breh dnaSa wiSkax kai haimanuta 'al ar'a?
But when the Son of man comes will he find faith on earth?

The parable of the Pharisee and the publican
L 18,9-14
trein gabrin slequ lhaikla lamcallayu
Two men went up to the temple to pray,
xad priSa waxrena maksa.
one a Pharisee and the other a tax collector.
whaw priSa qaem wa bainawhi lnapSeh whalen mcalle wa:
The Pharisee standing by himself was praying thus:
alaha mawdde-na lak dla weit ak Sarka dnaSa:
God, I thank you that I am not like other people:
xatope w'alobe wgaiyare dla ak hana maksa:
thieves, rogues, adulterers or even like this tax collector.
ca'em-na trein bSabbta wam'assar-na kollmiddem dqane-na.
I fast twice a week, I give a tenth of all my income.
haw den maksa qa'em wa min ruxqa wla cabe wa apla
But the tax collector standing far off would not even
'ainawhi irim laSmaiya ella Tarep wa 'al xadyeh wamar:
lift up his eyes to heaven, but beat his breast saying:
alaha xunaini lxaTTaiya!
God, be merciful to me. a sinner!
amar-na lkon danxet hana mzaddaq lbaiteh
I tell you, this man went down justified to his house
yattir min haw priSa.
rather than that Pharisee.
kollnaS ger dairim napSeh itmakkak
for everyone who exalts himself will be humbled,
wkoll man dyammek napSeh itrim.
but he humbles himself will be exalted.

The children
L 18,15 Mt 19,13 M 10,13
Sboqu Tlaye atein lwati wla tiklon innon
Let the little children come to me and do not stop them,
ddailen ger dak halen innon iteh malkuta daSmaiya.
for to such as these belongs the kingdom of heaven.
amen amar-na lkon dkoll dla iqabbel malkuta dalaha
Truly, I tell you, whoever does not receive the kingdom of God
ak Talya la ye"ol lah.
as a little child will not enter it.

The rich young man

L 18,18 Mt 19,16 M 10,17

mana qare att li Taba?
Why do you call me good?
lait Taba ella in xad alaha.
No one is good but God alone.
in den cabe att dte'ol lxaiye: Tar puqdane.
But if you wish to enter into life, keep the commandments.
puqdana yad'a att:
You know the commandments:
la tiqTol wla tgur
'You shall not kill and you shall not commit adultery
wla tignob wla tashed sahadut Suqra
and you shall not steal and you shall not bear false witness
wyaqqar labuk wlimmak
and honor your father and your mother
wtaxeb lqarribak ak napSak.
and love your neighbor as yourself.'
xada xassira lak: in cabe att gmira lmehwa
There is still one thing lacking: if you wish to be perfect,
zel zabben qinyanak whab lmiskene
go sell your possessions and give to the poor
wtihwe lak simta baSmaiya wta batari.
and you will have a treasure in heaven and come follow me.

On riches

L 18,24-29 Mt 19,23-29 M 10,23

amen amar-na lkon d'atla-y l'attira dye"ol
Truly, I say to you that it is hard for a rich man to enter
lmalkut Smaiya.
the kingdom of heaven.
tub den amar-na lkon dadlil-u lgamla lme"al baxrora
Again I say to you that it is easier for a camel to enter into the eye
damhaTTa aw 'attire dye"ol lmalkuta dalaha.
of the needle than for a rich man to enter the kingdom of God.
lwat bnainaSa hade la miSkxa
With men this is not possible
lwat alaha den kollmiddem miSkxa:
but with God everything is possible.
amen amar-na lkon datton dettaiton batari
Truly I say to you that you who have come to follow me
b'alma xadta ma dyeteb breh dnaSa 'al tronos
in the new world when the Son of man sits upon the throne
dSubxeh titbun ap atton 'al tre'asar kursawwan
of his glory you also will sit upon twelve seats

126

watdunun tre'asar SabTe disrayel.
and you will judge the twelve tribes of Israel.
wkollnaS dSabeq batte aw axe aw axwata aw aba
And anyone who leaves houses or brothers or sisters or father
aw imma aw attta aw bnaiya aw qurya miTTol Semi
or mother or wife or children or fields for the sake of my name,
xad bma' iqabbel wxaiye dal'alam yerat.
will receive a hundredfold and inherit eternal life.
saggiye den qadmaye dihwon xraye waxraye qadmaye.
But many who are first will be last and the last first.

The healing of the blind Bartimaeus
L 18,40-42
mana cabe att e'bbed lak?
What do you want me to do for you?
xazi! haimanutak axyatak.
Be seeing! Your faith has saved you.

Zacchaeus
L 19,1-10
istarhab xot zakkai yawmana ger wale dabbaitak ehwe.
Zacchaeus, hurry come down, for today I must stay at your house.
yawmana hawau xaiye lbaita hana
Today salvation has come to this house,
miTTol dap hana breh dabraham.
because he too is a son of Abraham.
etta ger breh dnaSa dyeb 'e wyaxxe haw middem dabbid wa.
For the Son of man came to seek and to save what was lost.

The parable of the minas
L 19,12-27
gabra xad bar Tohma rabba ezal latra raxxiqa
A certain man, a son of great nobility, went to a far country
dissab leh malkuta wyehppoq.
to receive for himself a kingdom and return.
waqra 'esra 'abdawhi wyab lhon 'esra mnin
And he called ten of his servants and gave them ten minas
wemar lhon: ittaggaru 'ad ate-na.
and said to them: 'Do business until I come back.'
bnay mditteh den sanein waw leh wSaddaru izgadde batreh
But the citizens hated him and sent a delegation after him,
wamrin: la cabein nan dyamlek 'alain hana.
saying: 'We do not want this man to rule over us.'
wkad nsab malkuta wahapaq emar:
And when he received the kingdom and returned, he told

diqron leh hanon 'abdawhi dyab lkon kespa
to call these servants to whom he gave money,
didda' mana xad xad minnhon ittaggar.
to learn what they had each gained by trading.
wetta qadmaya wemar: mari manyak 'esra mnin awttar
The first came saying: 'Lord, your mina has made ten more minas.'
amar leh: ew 'abda Taba, dabqallil
He told him: 'Well done, good servant! Because in a small thing
iSkaxt mhaiman tihwe SalliT 'al 'esra karkin.
you have been faithful, take charge of ten talents.'
wetta datrein wemar: mari manyak xammSa mnin 'abad.
The second came saying: 'Lord, your mina has made five minas.'
amar ap lhana: ap att tihwe SalliT 'al xammSa karkin.
He said to him also: 'You too take charge of five talents.'
wetta xrena wemar: mari ha manyak haw dit wa lwati
Then the other came, saying: 'Lord, here is your mina,
kad sim bsidona dexlet ger minnak
which I put in a cloth, for I was afraid of you,
dgabra att qaSya wSaqel att middem dla samt
because you are a harsh man, you take what you did not put in
wxaced att middem dla zer'et.
and reap what you did not sow.'
amar leh: min pumak eddunak
He said to him: 'Out of your own mouth I will judge you,
'abda biSa yada' wait li dgabra-na qaSya
you wicked servant, you knew that I am a harsh man,
wSaqel-na middem dla samet wxaced-na middem dla zer'et
taking what I did not put in and reaping what I did not sow.
Imana la yabt kespi 'al patora?
Why then you did not put my money into the bank?
wana ate weit wtaba' leh 'al ribbyateh:
Then when I returned, I could have collected it with interest.'
walhanon dqaimin qdamawhi emar: sabu minneh manya
He said to the bystanders: 'Take the mina from him
whabu lhaw dit lwateh 'esra mnin.
and give it to one who has ten minas.
amar-na lkon: dalkoll man dit leh itiheb leh
I tell you that to everyone who has, more will be given,
wmin haw den dlait leh ap haw dit leh itnseb minneh.
but from one who has not, even what he has will be taken away.
bram lhanon b'eldbabai ailen dla cbau damlek 'alaihon
But these enemies of mine who did not want me to reign over them,
aittau innon wqaTTelu innon qdamai.
bring them here and slaughter them in my presence.'

On marriage

Mt19,4-12 M10,2-12

la qraiton dhaw da'abad min braSit
Have you not read that he who created from the beginning
dikra wniqbeta 'abad innon wemar:
made them male and female and said:
miTTol hana iSboq gabra labuhi wlimmeh
'Because of this a man shall leave his father and mother
wiqqap lattteh wihwon traihon xad bsar.
and shall be joined to his wife and the two shall be one flesh.'
maden la wau trein ella xad pgar.
So they are no longer two, but one body.
middem hakel dalaha zaweg barnaSa la ipareS.
Therefore what God has joined together, let no one separate.
muSe luqbal qaSyut libbkon appes lkon
Moses because of hardness of your hearts allowed you
dtiSron niSSaikon:
to divorce your wives,
min braSit den la wa hakanna.
but from the beginning it was not so.
amar-na lkon den dman dSabeq attteh dla gawra
But I say to you, whoever divorces his wife, except for adultery,
wnaseb xreta ga'ar.
and marries another commits adultery.
wman naseb Sbiqta ga'ar.
and whoever marries a divorcee commits adultery.
la kollnaS sapeq lah lmillta hade ella man dihib leh.
Not all can accept this word but only those to whom it is given.
it ger mhaimne dmin karsa dimmhon itiledu hakanna
For there are eunuchs from their mother's womb born so
wit mhaimne dmin bnainaSa hawau mhaimne
and there are eunuchs who were made eunuchs by others,
wit mhaimne dhinnon 'abdaw napSehon mhaimne
and there are eunuchs who made themselves eunuchs
miTTol malkuta daSmaiya.
for the sake of the kingdom of heaven.
man dmiSkax disppaq isppaq.
He who is able to comprehend it, let him comprehend.

129

The parable of the workers in the vineyard
Mt20,1-16

damya ger malkuta daSmaiya Igabra mare baita
For the kingdom of heaven is like a man, a landowner,

danpaq bcapra dyegor pa'le Ikarmeh
who went out in the morning to hire workers for his vineyard.

qac ger 'am pa'le 'al deinara byawma
Having agreed with the workers for a denarius a day

wSaddar innon Ikarmeh.
he sent them into his vineyard.

wanpaq batlat Sa'in waxaza xrane dqaimin
When he went out at the third hour he saw others standing

bSuqa wbaTTilin wemar Ikon:
in the marketplace and idling, he said to them:

zelu ap atton Ikarma wmiddem dwale yaheb-na Ikon.
'You also go into the vineyard and what is right I will give you.'

hinnon den ezalu.
So they went off.

wanpaq tub bSet wbatSa' Sa'in wa'abad hakwat.
Again he went at the sixth and the ninth hour and did the same.

wlappai xada'esre Sa'in npaq weSkax xrane
And around the eleventh hour he went out and found others

dqaimin wbaTTilin wemar lhon:
who were standing idle and said to them:

mana qaimin atton yawma kulleh wbaTTilin?
'Why are standing here all day and idling?'

amrin leh: dla naS agran.
They said to him: 'Because no one has hired us.'

amar lhon: zelu ap atton Ikarma
He said to them: 'You also go into the vineyard

wmiddem dwale yasbin atton.
and what is right you will receive.'

kad hawa den ramSa emar mare karma Irabb baiteh:
When evening came, the owner of the vineyard said to his manager:

qri pa'le whab lhon agirhon
Call the workers and give them their pay,

wSarra min xrane wa'adamma Iqadmaye.
beginning with the last and ending with the first.

wettau hannon daxada'esre Sa'in: nsabu deinar deinar:
When those of the eleventh hour came, each received a denarius.

wkad ettau qadmaye sbaru dyattir Saqlin:
Now when the first came, they thought they would receive more

waSqalu deinar deinar ap hinnon.
but each of them also received a denarius.

wkad Sqalu rTanu 'al mare baita
And when they received it, they grumbled against the landowner.

wamrin: halen xraye xada Sa'a 'abadu
saying: 'These last worked only one hour, and you made
waSwitt innon 'amman daSqaln yuqreh dyawma wxumeh.
them equal to us who bore the burden of the day and its heat.'
hu den 'ana wemar lxad minnhon:
But he replied to one of them:
xaberi la ma'wel-na bak
'My friend, I am doing you no wrong,
la wa bdeinar qact 'ammi?
did you not agree with me for a denarius?
sab dilak wzel: cabe-na den dalhana xraya etten
Take what is yours and go, for I want to give to this last
ak dlak aw la SalliT li middem dcabe-na e'bbed
the same as you or am I not allowed to do what I want
bdili aw 'ainak biSa dana Tab-na?
with what is my own or is your eye evil because I am good?'
hakanna ihwon xraye qadmaye wqadmaye xraye.
So the last will be first, and the first will be last.
saggi'in innon ger qraiya waz'orin gbaiya.
For many are called but few are chosen.

The raising of Lazarus

J11,1-24

hana kurhana la wa dmawta ella xalap tiSboxta dalaha
This illness is not unto death, but it is for the glory of God,
diStabbax breh dalaha miTTolateh.
so that the Son of God may be glorified through it.
tau nezal tub layhud.
Let us go to Judea again.
la tart'esre Sa'in it byawma?
Are there not twelve hours in a day?
win naS mhallek bimama la mitteqel
If one walks during the day, he does not stumble,
miTTol dxaze nuhareh d'alma hana.
because he sees the light of this world.
in naS den blilya ihallek mitteqel
But if one walks at night, he stumbles
miTTol dnuhara lait beh.
because the light is not in him.
la'azar raxman Skeb: ella azel-na da'iriwhi.
Lazarus our friend is asleep, but I am going to wake him up.
la'azar mit leh: wxade-na dla weit tamman miTTolatkon
Lazarus is dead; I am glad I was not there for your sake
dathaimnun: ella halleku ltamman!
so that you may believe. But let us go there!

I am the resurrection

qa'em axuki.
Your brother will rise again.
ana-na nuxama wxaiye:
I am the resurrection and the life;
man daihaimen bi
whoever believes in me,
apin imut ixxe
even if he dies, will live,
wkoll dxai wamhaimen bi
and everyone who lives and believes in me
l'alam la imut.
will never die.
mhaimna atti hade?
Do you believe this?
aika samtonaihi?
Where have you laid him?
Sqolu kepa hade!
Take away that stone!
la emret leki din thaimnin
Did I not tell you that if you believe
texzein Subxeh dalaha?
you will see the glory of God?
aba mawdde-na lak daSma'tani:
Father, I thank you that you have heard me.
wana yada'-na dabkollzban Sama' att li
I know that you always hear me,
ella miTTol kinSa hana dqa'em amar-na halen
but because of the crowd standing here I have said this,
daihaimnun datt Saddartani.
so that they may believe that you sent me.
la'azar ta Ibar!
Lazarus, come out!
Srawhi waSboqu azel!
Unbind him, and let him go!

133

The third prediction of the passion

Mt20,17 L18,31

ha salqinan loriSlem wmiSttalman kullhen
See, we are going up to Jerusalem and everything will be fulfilled
daktiban banbiyye 'al breh dnaSa.
that is written by the prophets about the Son of man.
miStlem ger Irabbai kahane walsapre
For he will handed over to the chief priests and the scribes
waixaiyebunaihi Imawta
and they will condemn him to death
waiSilmunaihi l'amme waibazxun beh
and they will hand him over to the Gentiles and they will mock him,
wainagdunaihi wayazqapunaihi
they will beat him and crucify him
walyawma datlata iqum.
and on the third day he will rise again.

The sons of Zebedee

Mt20,20 M10,35

mana cabya atti?
What do you want?
la yad'in-tton mana Salin-tton:
You do not know what you are asking;
miSkxin-tton ImiSta kasa dana 'atid ImiSta
are you able to drink the cup that I am about to drink
aw ma'modita dana 'amed-na te'emdun?
or to be baptized with the baptism with which I am baptized?
kasi tiSton ma'modita dana 'amed-na
You will drink my cup, with the baptism that I am baptized with
te'emdun dtibun den min yammini wmin semmali
you will be baptized, but to sit on my right hand and on my left,
la hawat dili detten ella lailen
is not mine to grant, but to those
ditTaiyabat min abi.
for whom it has been prepared by my Father.
yad'in atton dreSaihon d'amme maraihon innon
You know that the rulers of the Gentiles are their lords
wrawrebanaihon SalliTin 'alaihon:
and their nobles rule over them;
la den hakanna ihwe bainatkon
it will not be so among you,
ella man dcabe bkon dihwe rabba ihwe Ikon mSamSana
but who wishes among you to be great must be your servant,
wman dcabe bkon dihwe qadmaya ihwe Ikon 'abda.
and whoever wishes to be first among you must be your slave.

aikanna dabreh dnaSa la etta diStammaS
Just as the Son of man did not come to be served
ella daiSammeS waditten napSeh purqana xalap saggiye.
but to serve, and to give his life a ransom for many.

The anointing at Bethany

J12,1-8 Mt26,6 M14,3

Sboqeh mana malein atton lah lattta?
Leave her alone. Why do you trouble the woman?
'abada Sappira 'ebdat lwati:
She has done a beautiful deed to me,
bkullzban ger miskene it lkon 'ammkon
for you have always the poor with you,
li den la bkullzban it lkon.
but me not always you will have.
hade den darmyat besma hana 'al guSmi
When she poured this perfume over my body,
ak damiqbrani 'ebdat.
she has prepared me for burial.
wamen amar-na lkon daika dtitqrez sbarti haze
Truly I tell you, wherever this good news is proclaimed
bkulleh 'alma itmallal ap middem d'ebdat hade ldukranah.
in the whole world, will be told what she did in memory of her.

The triumphal entry

Mt21,1-16 M11,1-10 L19,28-40

zelu laqrita hade dluqbalkon wmixda miSkxin
Go to this village in front of you and right away you will find
xamara dassira w'ila 'ammah Srau attau li.
a donkey tied and a colt with her, untie them and bring to me.
win naS amar lkon middem
If anyone says to you anything,
emar leh dalmaran mitbe'ein
tell him that our Lord needs them
wmixda mSaddar lhon lka.
and immediately he will send them here.
amar-na lkon din halen iStqun kepe iqi'yan.
I tell you, if these were silent, the very stones would cry out.
en mimtom la qraiton:
Yes, have you never read:
dmin puma daTlaye wadyallude
'Out of the mouth of babes and infants
taqqent tiSboxta.
you have prepared a praise.'

The lament for Jerusalem

L 19,41-44

illu kai ida'ti ailen ditaihen daSlameki apin bhana yawmeki!
If you only knew the things that make for peace on this day!
haSa den itkassi lhen min 'anaiki.
But now they are hidden from your eyes.
yeton leki den yawmata
For the days will come upon you
dyexdruneki b'eldbabaiki
when your enemies will surround
wyeleuneki min koll dukka.
and hem you in on all sides.
wisixpuneki wlabanaiki bgawweki
And they crush you and your children within you
wla iSbqun beki kep 'al kep
and they will not leave in you one stone upon another,
xalap dla ida'ti zabna dsu'raneki.
because you did not recognize the time of your visitation.

The second cleansing of the temple

Mt21,10 M11,11 L19,45

ktib-u dbaiti bet clota itiqre:
It is written: 'My house shall be called a house of prayer,'
atton den 'abadtonaihi m'arta dlisTaye.
but you are making it a den of robbers.

The fig tree cursed

Mt21,18 M11,12

la ihwon beki tub pere l'alam!
May no fruit ever come from you again!
amen amar-na Ikon din tihwe bkon haimanuta wla titpalgun
Truly I tell you, if you have faith and do not doubt,
la balxod hade dtetta te'bdun
not only will you do this to the fig tree
ella apen ITura hana temrun:
but even if you say to this mountain:
diStaqel wpel byamma: tihwe.
'Be lifted up and thrown into the sea,' it will be done.
wkollmiddem dtiSilun baclota wathaimnun tissbun.
Whatever you ask for in prayer and believe it, you will receive.

136

By what authority? To the priests

Mt21,24-27 M11,29

eSa'elkon ap ana millta xada win temrun li
I will also ask you one question; if you tell me the answer,
ap ana amar-na Ikon baina SulTana halen 'abed.
then I will also tell you by what authority I do these things.
ma'moditeh dyoxannan min aimikka iteh:
Where was John's baptism from?
min Smaiya aw min bnainaSa?
Was it from heaven or from men?
apla ana amar-na Ikon baina SulTana halen 'abed-na.
Neither will I tell you by what authority I am doing these things.

The parable of two sons

Mt21,28-32

mana den mitixze Ikon?
Now what do you think?
gabra xad it wa leh bnaiya trein waqreb lwat qadmaya
A man had two sons and he went to the first
wemar leh: beri zel yawmana plox bkarma.
and said to him: 'Son, go and work in the vineyard today.'
hu den 'ana wemar: la cabe-na.
He answered saying: 'I will not.'
bxarta den ittwi wezal.
But later he regretted it and went.
waqreb lwat xrena wemar leh hakwat:
Then he went to the other and said to him likewise.
hu den 'ana wemar: ana mari wla ezal.
And he answered saying: 'I will, sir': but he did not go.
mana min halen traihon 'abad cibyana dabuhi?
Which one of these two did the will of his father?
amen amar-na Ikon dmakse wzanyata
Truly I tell you, the tax collectors and the prostitutes
qadmin Ikon Imalkuta dalaha.
are going ahead of you into the kingdom of God.
etta ger lwatkon yoxannan burxa dzaddiquta wla
For John came to you the way of righteousness and you did not
haimentonaihi: makse den wzanyata haimenuhi.
believe him, but the tax collectors and the prostitutes believed him.
atton den apla kad xazaiton
And even when you saw it,
ittwitton bxarta dathaimenun beh.
you did not later change your minds and believe him.

The parable of the tenants

Mt21,33-46 L20,8-19

Sma'u xrena matla:
Hear another parable:

gabra xad it wa mare baita wancab karma
There was a man landowner who planted a vineyard,

waxdreh syaga waxapar beh ma'carta wabna beh magdla
put a fence around it, dug a wine press in it and built a tower in it.

wawxdeh lpallaxe waxazaq.
Then he leased it to tenants, and went on a journey.

kad den mTa zabna dpere: Saddar l'abdawhi
When the harvest time had come, he send his servants

lwat pallaxe daySaddrun leh min pere dkarmeh.
to the tenants to collect from the produce of the vineyard.

wexxadu pallaxe l'abdawhi
But the tenants seized his servants,

wit damxawhi wit dragmuhi wit dqaTluhi.
and beat one, another they stoned , and killed another.

wtub Saddar 'abde xrane dsaggiyin min qadmaye:
Again he sent other servants, more than the first,

whakwat 'abadu lhon.
and likewise they did to them.

xrayat den Saddar lwathon labreh kad amar:
Finally he sent his son to them, saying:

kbar ibihton min beri.
Perhaps they will respect my son.

pallaxe den kad xazawhi labra amru bainathon:
But when the tenants saw the son, they said to themselves:

hanaw yarta: tau niqTeliwhi wnexod yartuteh.
This is the heir; come, let us kill him and seize his inheritance.

wexxadu appquhi labar min karma wqaTluhi.
So they seized him, threw him out of vineyard and killed him.

ma detta hakel mareh dkarma
Now when comes the owner of the vineyard,

mana ye'bbed lpallaxe hanon?
what will he do to those tenants?

la mimmtom qraiton baktaba:
have you never read in the scriptures:

dkepa dasliyu bannaye hi hawat lreSa dzawita
The stone that the builders rejected has become the cornerstone,

min lawat marya hade witeh tadmurta b'ainain?
by the Lord has this been done, and it is wonderful in our eyes?

miTTol hana amar-na lkon dtiStqel minnkon malkuta dalaha
Therefore I tell you: The kingdom of God will be taken away from you

139

wtitiheb l'amma d'abed pere.
and given to a people who are producing fruit.
wman dippel 'al kepa hade itid'a':
The one who falls on this stone will be broken to pieces,
wkoll dhi tippel 'alawhi tidrewhi.
and on whom it falls will be crushed.

The parable of the marriage banquet
Mt22,1-14

itdamyat malkuta daSmaiya lgabra malka
The kingdom of heaven may be compared to a man, a king,
da'abad miStuta labreh:
who gave a wedding banquet for his son.
wSaddar l'abdawhi diqrun lamzamne lmiStuta:
He sent his servants to call those invited to the wedding banquet,
wla cbau lmeta.
but they would not come.
wtub Saddar 'abde xrane wemar: emmaru lamzamne
Again he sent other servants, saying: Tell those invited:
dha Saruti mTaiyaba wtawrai wampaTmai qTilin
'Look, my dinner is prepared, my oxen and fat calves are killed,
wkollmiddem mTaiyab tau lmiStuta.
and everything is ready; come to the wedding banquet.'
hanon den bsau wezalu it dlaqriteh
But they ignored it and went away, one to his farm,
wit daltegurteh Sarka den axxadu l'abdawhi
another to his business, the rest seized his servants
wca"aru wqaTTelu.
mistreated them and killed them.
kad Sma' den malka rgez wSaddar xailawateh:
When the king heard of it, he was enraged and sent his troops,
awbbed lqaTole hanon wlamditthon awqed.
destroyed those murderers and burned their city.
haiden emar l'abdawhi: miStuta mTaiyeba:
The he said to his servants: 'The banquet is ready
whanon damzamnin wau la Swein wau.
but those invited were not worthy.
zelu hakel lmapqane durxata wkollman dmiSkxin-tton
Go therefore into main streets, and everyone you find
qrau lmiStuta.
invite to the wedding banquet.'
wanpaqu 'abade hanon lurxata wkanneSu koll diSkaxu
Those servants went into the streets and gathered all they found,
biSe wTabe witimli beit miStuta smike.
both bad and good; so the wedding hall was filled with guests.

w'al malka dyexze smike waxaza tamman gabra
But when the king came in to see the guests, he saw a man there
dla IbiS IbuSa dmiStuta wemar leh:
who was not wearing a wedding robe, and he said to him:
xaberi aikanna 'alett Ika kad naxte dmiStuta lait lak?
'Friend, how did you get in here without a wedding robe?'
hu den iStattaq.
And he was speechless.
haiden emar malka lamSamSane:
Then the king said to the attendants:
assoru idawhi wriglawhi wappquhi IxeSSoka baraya.
'Bind him hand and foot, and throw him into the outer darkness.'
tamman ihwe bikya wxuraq Sinne.
There will be weeping and gnashing of teeth.
saggiyin innon ger qraiya waz'orin gbaiya.
For many are called, but few are chosen.

Tribute to Caesar

Mt22,15-22 M12,13-17 L20,20-26

mana mnassein-tton li nasbai bappe?
Why are you testing me, you hypocrites?
xawwauni deinara dksep reSa.
Show me the denarius of the head tax.
dmannu calma hana waktaba?
Whose image is this whose inscription?
habu hakel dqesar Iqesar
Then give what is Caesar's to Caesar
wdalaha lalaha.
and what is God's to God.

About the resurrection

Mt22,29 M12,18 L20,27

Ta'ein-tton dla yad'in-tton ktabe
You are wrong because you know neither the scriptures
wla xaileh dalaha:
nor the power of God.
baqyamta ger dmite la nasbin niSSe ap la niSSe hawyan Igabre
For in the resurrection they neither marry nor are given in marriage
ella ak malake dalaha baSmaiya itaihon.
but are like angels of God in heaven.
'al qyamta den dmite la qraiton middem ditamar
But as for resurrection of the dead, have you not read what was said
Ikon min alaha demar:
to you by God, saying:

141

dana-na alaheh dabraham alaheh disxaq alaheh dya'qob?
'I am the God of Abraham, the God of Isaac, the God of Jacob?'
walaha la hawa dmite ella dxaiye.
He is God not of the dead, but of the living.

The first commandment

Mt22,37-40 M12,29-34 L10,27

qadmay min kullhon puqdane:
The first of all commandments is:
Sma' israyel marya alahan marya xad-u:
'Hear, o Israel, the Lord our God the Lord is one;
wadtirxam lmarya alahak min kulleh libbak
you shall love the Lord your God with all your heart
wmin kullah napSah wmin kulleh re'yanak
and with all your soul and with all your mind
wmin kulleh xailak:
and all your strength,'
hanaw puqdana rabba wqadmaya.
this is the greatest and first commandment.
wdatrein ddame leh:
And a second is like it:
dtirxam lqarribak ak napSak.
'You shall love your neighbor as yourself.'
bhalen trein puqdanin talya oraita wanbiyye.
On these two commandments hang the law and the prophets.
la hawait raxxiq min malkuta dalaha.
You are not far from the kingdom of God.
trica'it emart: hade 'abed wtixxe.
You have answered right; do this and you will live.

David's son

Mt22,41-46 L20,41-44

mana amrin atton 'al maSixa bar mannu?
What do you say about the Messiah? Whose son is he?
waikanna dawid brux qare leh marya?
How is it then that David in the Spirit calls him Lord?
emar ger: demar marya lmari dteb lak min yammini
For he said: 'The Lord said to my Lord: Sit at my right hand,
'adamma desim b'eldbabaik taxet riglaik:
until I put your enemies under your feet.'
in hakel dawid qare leh marya aikanna breh-u?
If David then calls him Lord, how can he be his son?

142

Scribes and Pharisees denounced

Mt23,1-12 L20,45

'al kursya dmuSe itebu sapre wapriSe:
On the chair of Moses are seated the scribes and Pharisees;
koll middem hakel dyemrun lkon dtiTTrun Tarru wa'abedu
therefore all they tell you to observe, observe and do,
ak 'abadaihon den la te'bbdun:
but after their deeds do not do:
amrin ger wla 'abdin.
for they say, but are not doing.
wasrin mawble yaqqirata
They tie up heavy burdens
wsaimin 'al katpata dabnainaSa
and lay them on men's shoulders,
hinnon den bcebe'hon la cabein diqirbun lahen.
but they themselves would not lift a finger to move them.
wkullhon 'abadaihon 'abdin ditixzon labnainaSa
And they do all their deeds to be seen by the people,
maptein ger tiplaihon wmawrekin tiklata dmarTuTaihon.
fcr they make their phylacteries broad and their tassels long.
wraxmin reS smake baxSamaita wreS mawtbe
They love places of honor at banquets and seats of honor
baknuSata waSlama bSuqe
in the synagogues and greetings in marketplaces
wadihwon mitiqrein min naSa rabbi.
and being called by the people Rabbi.
atton den la titiqron rabbi
But you should not be called Rabbi,
xad-u ger rabbkon: atton den kullhon axe atton.
for you have but one teacher, and you all are brothers.
waba la tiqron lkon bar'a:
And call no one your father on earth,
xad-u ger abukon dbaSmaiya.
for one is your Father, the one in heaven.
wla titiqron mdabbrane
And do not be called Masters,
miTTol dxad-u mdabbrankon mSixa.
for one is your Master, the Messiah.
haw den drab bkon ihwe lkon mSamSana.
The greatest among you will be your servant.
man ger dairim napSeh imakkak:
Whoever exalts himself will be humbled,
wman dyammek napSeh ittrim.
and whoever humbles himself will be exalted.

Woes to the scribes and Pharisees

Mt23,13-36 L20,47

wai lkon sapre wapriSe nasbai bappe!
Woe to you, scribes and Pharisees, hypocrites!
daklin-tton batte darmlata b'ilta dmawrekin-tton clawatkon:
Who devour widows' houses and on pretense make long prayers.
miTTol hana tqabblun dina yattira.
Because of this you will receive greater condemnation.
wai lkon sapre wapriSe nasbai bappe!
Woe to you, scribes and Pharisees, hypocrites!
daxidin-tton malkuta daSmaiya qdam bnainaSa:
For you lock people out of the kingdom of heaven.
atton ger la 'a'elin-tton wlailen d'a'elin la Sabqin-tton lme"al.
You do not go in yourselves and do not let those entering to go in.
wai lkon sapre wapriSe nasbai bappe!
Woe to you, scribes and Pharisees, hypocrites!
dmitkarkin-tton yamma wyabSa dte'bdun xad giyora
For you cross sea and land to make a single convert,
wma dahawa 'abdin-tton leh brah dgehanna
And when it happens you make him a son of hell
a'pa 'alaikon.
twice as much as yourselves.
wai lkon nagode smaiya damrin-tton dman dyame
Woe to you, blind guides, who say that whoever swears
bhaikla la wa middem man den dyame
by the temple, that is nothing, but whoever swears
bdahaba dabhaikla xa'eb.
by the gold of the temple is obligated.
sakle wasmaiya! mana ger rabb
You blind fools! For which is greater,
dahaba aw haikla dhu mqaddeS leh ldahaba?
the gold or the temple that made the gold sacred?
wman dyame bmadbxa la wa middem
And whoever swears by the altar, that is nothing,
man den dyame bqurbana dal'el minneh xa'eb.
but whoever swears by the gift on it, is obligated.
sakle wa'wire mana rabb qurbana
You blind fools! For which is greater, the gift
aw madbxa damqaddeS lqurbana?
or the altar that makes the gift sacred?
man dyame hakel bmadbxa yame beh
So whoever swears by the altar, swears by it
wabkoll ma dit l'el minneh.
and by everything that's on it.

144

wman dyame hakel bhaikla yame beh
and whoever swears by the temple, swears by it
wabman d'amar beh.
and by one who dwells in it.
wman dyame baSmaiya yame bkursyeh dalaha
And whoever swears by heaven, swears by the throne of God
wabman dyateb l'el minneh.
and by the one who is seated on it.
wai lkon sapre wapriSe nasbai bappe!
Woe to you, scribes and Pharisees, hypocrites!
dam'assrin-tton nan'a waSbetta wkammuna waSbaqton
For you tithe mint, dill and cumin, and have neglected
yaqqirateh doraita: dina waxanana whaimanuta.
weightier things of the law: justice and mercy and faith.
hade den wale wa dte'bdun whalen la tiSbqun.
These things you should have done without neglecting the others.
nagode smaiya damcallin baqqe wbal'in gamle!
You blind guides! You strain out a gnat but swallow a camel!
wai lkon sapre wapriSe nasbai bappe!
Woe to you, scribes and Pharisees, hypocrites!
damdakkein atton lbareh dkasa wad zabora
For you clean the outside of cup and dish,
lgaww den malein haTupya w'awla.
but inside they are full of greed and iniquity.
priSe 'awire! dakkau luqdam gawweh dkasa wadzabora
You blind Pharisees! First clean the inside of the cup and dish,
dahawa ap barhon dke.
so that the outside also may become clean.
wai lkon sapre wapriSe nasbai bappe!
Woe to you, scribes and Pharisees, hypocrites!
ddamein-tton lqabre makilSe dmin lbar mitixzein Sappire
For you are like whitewashed tombs, which on the outside look nice,
min lgaww den mlein garme dmite wkullah Tannputa.
but inside they are full of the bones of the dead and all filth.
hakanna ap-tton min lbar mitixzein-tton labnainaSa ak zaddiqe
So you too on the outside look righteous to the people,
wmin lgaww mlein-tton 'awla wmassab bappe.
but inside you are full of evildoing and hypocrisy.
wai lkon sapre wapriSe nasbai bappe!
Woe to you, scribes and Pharisees, hypocrites!
dbanein-tton qabre danbiyye wamcabbtin-tton beit qbure
For you build the tombs of the prophets and adorn the monuments
dzaddiqe wamrin-tton:
of the righteous, and you say:

145

dillu hawain byawmai abahain la hawein wain
'If we had lived in the days of our fathers, we would not have
Ihon Sawtape badma danbiyye.
taken part with them in the blood of the prophets.'
maden masihdin-tton 'al napSkon dabnaiya atton
Thus you testify against yourselves that you are the children
dhanon dqaTTelu lanbiyye.
of those who murdered the prophets.
wap atton mallau mSuxta dabahaikon!
You too fill up the measure of your fathers!
xawawata! yalda dakedne!
You snakes! you brood of vipers!
aikanna te'erqun min dina dgehanna?
How are you to escape the damnation of hell?
miTTol hana ana mSaddar-na lwatkon
For this reason, I send to you
nbiyye wxakkime wsapre:
prophets, sages and scribes;
minnhon qaTlin-tton wzapqin-tton wminnhon mnagdin-tton
some of whom you will kill and crucify, and some you will flog
baknuSatkon wtirdpun innon min mdina lamdina
in your synagogues and pursue them from town to town,
aikanna dyete 'alaikon kulleh dma dzaddiqe diteSed 'al ar'a
so that upon you may come all the righteous blood shed on earth,
min dmeh dhabel zaddiqa wa'adamma ladmeh dazqarya
from the blood of righteous Abel to the blood of Zachariah,
bar brakya haw daqTalton bainai haikla lmadbxa.
the son of Barachias, you killed between the temple and the altar.
amen amar-na lkon dyetyan halen kullhen 'al Sarbta hade.
Truly I tell you, all this will come upon this generation.

The widow's mite
L21,1-4 M12,41-44

amen amar-na lkon dhade armalta miskenta yattir
Truly I tell you, this poor widow put in more
min kullhon naSa dramein armyat beit gaza:
than all those people who are contributing to the treasury;
kullhon ger min middem dyattir Ihon armiyu
for they all contributed out of their surplus,
hade den min xassirutah kollmiddem dit wa lah armyateh
but she out of her poverty put in everything she had,
kulleh qinyanah.
her whole living.

Signs before the end

Mt24,1-8 M13,1-8 L21,5-11

la ha xazein atton halen kullhen?
You see all these things, do you not?
amen amar-na lkon dla tiStbeq harka kep 'al kep
Truly I tell you, not one stone will be left here upon another stone
dla tisttattar.
that will not be thrown down.
izdaru la naS yaT'eikon.
Beware that no one deceives you.
saggiye ger yeton bSemi wyemrun:
For many will come in my name, saying:
dana-na mSixa wsaggiye yaT'on:
'I am the Messiah,' and they will deceive many.
'atidin-tton den lmiSma' qerse wSim'a daqrabe.
You will hear of wars and rumors of wars.
xazau la titdawdun: wale ger dkullhen ihiwyan:
See that you are not alarmed, for all these things must happen,
ella la 'adakkel Sullama.
but it will not yet be the end.
iqum ger 'amma 'al 'amma wmalkuta 'al malkuta
For nation will rise against nation and kingdom against kingdom,
wihwon kapne wmawtane wzaw'e bdukka dukka.
there will be famines, plagues and earthquakes in various places.

Persecutions foretold

Mt24,9-14 M13,9 L21,12

halen den kullhen reSa innen dxeble.
All these are the beginning of pains.
haiden yaSilmunakon lulcawa wiqTilunakon
Then they will hand you over to persecution, and thcy will kill you
wtihwon sniin min kullhon 'amme miTTol Semi.
and you will be hated by all nations because of my name.
haiden itkaSlun saggiye wisnon xad lxad
Then many will fall away and will hate one another
wyaSilmun xad lxad.
and will betray one another.
wsaggiye nbiyye daggale iqumun wyaT'on lsaggiye.
And many false prophets will arise and deceive many.
wmiTTol saggiyut 'awla ipug xubba dsaggiye:
Because of the increase of evil, the love of many will grow cold.
man damsaibar den 'adamma lxarta hu ixxe.
But the one who endures to the end will be saved.
wtitkrez hade sbarta dmalkuta bkuleh 'alma
This gospel of the kingdom will be preached in the whole world

lsahaduta dkullhon 'amme: haiden yete Sullama.
as a testimony to all nations; and then the end will come.

The great tribulation

Mt24,15-22 M13,14-20 L21,20-24

ma den daxazaiton ata Tannpta dxurba
So when you see the sign of abomination of desolation
ditamar ddaniel nbiyya dqaima bdukkta qaddiSta:
as spoken of by Daniel the prophet, standing in the holy place,
haw dqare istakkal.
he who reads, let him understand.
haiden ailen dbayhud innon ye'erqun lTura whaw
Then those in Judea must flee to the mountains, and the one
dbiggara-w la ixxot lmissab dabbaiteh
on the housetop must not go down to get what is in the house,
waina dabxakla-w la itihpeq lbestreh lmissab lbaSeh.
And the one in the field must not turn back to get a coat.
wai den lbaTnata wlailen dmayinqan bhanon yawmata!
Woe to those who are pregnant and nursing in those days!
callau den dla ihwe 'aruqikon bsatwa wla bSabbta.
Pray that your flight may not be in winter or on a Sabbath.
ihwe ger haiden ulcana rabba aina dla hawa
For there will be a great tribulation such as has not been
min reSiteh d'alma wa'adamma lhaSa wla ihwe.
from the beginning of the world until now nor will ever be.
willu la itkariyu yawmata hanon la xaiye wa koll bsar:
And if those days had not been cut short, no flesh would be saved;
miTTol gbaiya den itkaron yawmata hanon.
but for the sake of the elect those days will be cut short.

False prophets

Mt 24,23-28 M13,21 L17,23

haiden in naS yemar lkon: ha harka-w mSixa
Then if anyone says to you: 'Look! Here is the Messiah!'
aw harka: la thaimnun.
or 'There he is!' - do not believe it.
iqumun ger mSixe daggale wanbiyye dkaddabuta
False messiahs and lying prophets will arise
wintnun atwata rawrbata ak dyaT'on
and they will produce great signs and wonders to mislead,
in miSkxa ap lagbaiya.
if possible, even the elect.
ha qadmet emret lkon.
See, beforehand I have told you.

in hakel yemrun lkon: ha bxurba-w la tipqun.
So, if they say to you: 'Look, he is in the desert,' do not go out.
aw dha btawwana-w la thaimnun.
Or: 'He is in the inner rooms,' do not believe it.
aikanna ger dbarqa napeq min madinxa wmitixze 'adamma
For as the lightning comes from the east and flashes as far as
lma'arba hakanna tihwe metiteh dabreh dnaSa.
the west, so will be the coming of the Son of man.
aika den dihwe pagra tamman itkanSun niSre.
Wherever corpse is, there the vultures will gather.

The coming of the Son of man
Mt24,29 M13,24 L21,25

mixda den batar ulcana dyawmata hanon SimSa
Immediately after the tribulation of those days the sun will be
yexSak wsahara la ixawwe nuhareh wkawkbe ipplun
darkened and the moon will not show its light and the stars will fall
min Smaiya wxaile daSmaiya ittzi'un.
from heaven, and powers of heaven will be shaken.
whaiden itixze niSeh dabreh dnaSa baSmaiya
Then the sign of the Son of man will appear in heaven,
whaiden yarqedan kullhen Sarbata dar'a
and then all the tribes of the earth will mourn,
wyexzun labreh dnaSa dete 'al 'ananai Smaiya
and they will see the Son of man coming on the clouds of heaven
'am xaila wSubxa saggiya.
with power and great glory.
waiSaddar malakawhi 'am Sipora rabba
And he will send out his angels with the loud trumpet
waikannSun lagbaiya dileh min arb'at ruxe
and they will gather his elect from the four winds,
min reShon daSmaiya wa'adamma lreShon.
from one end of heaven to the other end.

The time of the coming - the parable of the fig tree
Mt24,32-36 M13,28-32 L21,39-43

min tetta den illappu pelleta:
From the fig tree learn the lesson:
dmixda dsawkeh rakan wpar'in Tarpeh
As soon as its branches become tender and sprout leaves,
yad'in-tton damTa qaiTa.
you know that summer is near.
hakanna ap atton ma daxazaiton halen kullhen
So also, when you see all these things,

149

da'u damTat lah ltar'a.
know that he is near at the gates.
amen amar-na lkon dla te'bar Sarbta hade
Truly I tell you, this generation will not pass away
'adamma dhalen kullhen ihiwyan.
until all these things have taken place.
Smaiya war'a ye'brun wmillai la ye'brun.
Heaven and earth will pass away, but my words will not pass away.
'al yawma den haw w'al Sa'ta haw naS la yada'
But about that day and hour no one knows,
apla malake daSmaiya ella aba balxod.
not even the angels of heaven, but the Father alone.

The parable of the flood

Mt24,24-37 L17,26-36

aikanna den dyawmai nox
For as it was in the days of Noah,
hakanna tihwe metiteh dabreh dnaSa.
so will be the coming of the Son of man.
aikanna ger ditaihon wau qdam Tawpana aklin wSatein
For as it was before the flood, they were eating and drinking
wnasbin niSSe wayabbin lgabre 'adamma lyawma
marrying and giving in marriage, until the day
d'al nox lkewella wla ida'u 'adamma detta Tawpana
Noah entered the ark, and they knew nothing until the flood came
waSqal lkullhon:
and carried them all away,
hakanna tihwe metiteh dabreh dnaSa.
so too will be the coming of the Son of man.
haiden trein ihwon baqrita: xad itdbar wxad iStbeq.
Then two will be in the field, one will be taken and one will be left.
wtartein ihiwyan Taxnan braxya:
Two women will be grinding at the mill;
xada mitdabra wxada miStabqa.
one will be taken and one will be left.
itt'iru hakel dla yad'in-tton baida Sa'ta ate markon.
So be alert, for you do not know at what hour your Lord will come.
hade den da'u dillu yada' wa mare baita baida maTTarta
Know this: if the owner of the house knew at what time the thief
ate gannaba mitt'ir wa wla Sabeq wa ditipleS baiteh.
was coming, he would watch and not let his house to be plundered.
miTTol hana ap atton hawau mTaiyabin
Therefore you also must be ready,
dabSa'ta dla sabrin-tton yete breh dnaSa.
for at an hour you do not expect, the Son of man will come.

The parable of ten virgins

Mt25, 1-13

haiden tidme malkuta daSmaiya l'assar btulan
Then the kingdom of heaven will be like ten virgins,
hanen dansab lampedaihen wanpaq lura' xatna wkallta.
who took their lamps and went out to meet the groom and bride.
xammeS den minnhen xakkiman wai wxammeS saklan.
Five of them were wise and five were foolish.
whanen saklata nsab lampedaihen wla nsab 'ammhen miSxa.
The foolish ones took their lamps and did not take oil with them.
hanen den xakkimata nsab miSxa bmane 'am lampedaihen.
But the wise took flasks of oil with their lamps.
kad awxar den xatna nam kullhen wadmeq.
As the bridegroom was delayed, they all got drowsy and slept.
wabpilggeh dlilya hawat q'ata:
But at midnight there was a shout:
ha xatna: ate poqu lur'eh!
Look! Here is the bridegroom! Come out to meet him!
haiden qam kullhen btulata halen wtaqqen lampedaihen.
Then all those virgins got up and trimmed their lamps.
amran den hanen saklata lxakkimata:
Those foolish said to the wise:
habein lan min miSikxen dha d'eku lhon lampedain.
'Give us some of your oil, for our lamps are going out.'
'anai halen xakkimata wamran:
But the wise ones replied saying:
lma la ispaq lan walken.
'No, there will not be enough for us and for you.
ella zillein lwat ailen damzabbnin wazbinnein lken.
Go instead to the merchants and buy some for yourselves.'
wkad ezal lmizban etta xatna
While they went to buy, the bridegroom came
wailen danTaiyban way
and those who were ready
'al 'ammeh lbeit xalola wittxed tar'a.
went with him into the wedding hall and the door was shut.
bxarta den ettai ap hanen btulata xranyata wamran:
Later the other virgins came also, saying:
maran maran ptax lan! hu den 'ana wemar lahen:
'Lord, lord, open to us!' But he replied, saying to them:
amen amar-na lken dla yada'-na lken.
'Truly I tell you, I do not know you.'
itt'iru hakel dla yad'in-tton lyawma haw wla Sa'ta.
Be on the alert then, for you know neither the day nor the hour.

151

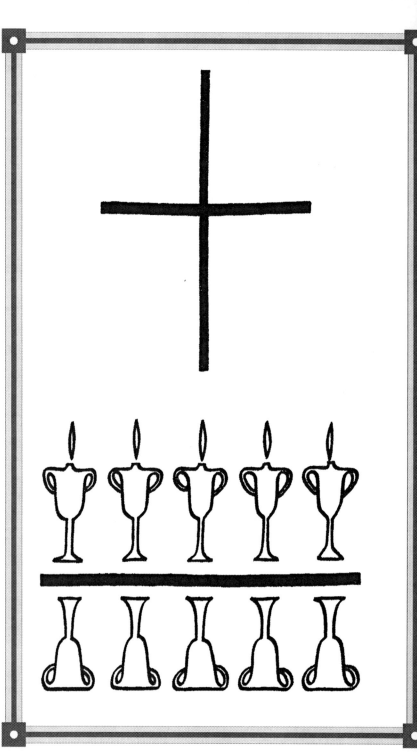

The parable of the talents

Mt25,14-30

ak gabra ger daxazaq qra l'abdawhi
Like a man going on a journey called his servants
waSlem lhon qinyaneh: it dyab leh xammeS kakrin
and entrusted to them his goods: to one he gave five talents,
wit dtartein wit daxada
and to another two and to another one,
naS naS ak xaileh: waxazaq mixda.
to each according to his ability. Then he went right away.
ezal den haw dansab xammeS kakrin ittagar bhen
The one who received five talents went and traded with them
witar xammeS xranyan:
and made five more talents.
whakwat ap haw dtartein ittagar tartein xranyan:
Likewise, the one who had two made two more.
haw den dansab xada ezal xapar bar'a wTaSSi
But one who had received one, dug in the ground and hid
kespa dmareh.
his master's money.
batar den zabna saggiya etta marhon d'abde hanon
After a long time the master of those servants came
wansab minnhon xuSbana.
and settled accounts with them.
waqreb haw dansab wa xammeS kakrin wqareb
The one who had received five talents came up and brought
xammeS xranyan wemar: mari xammeS kakrin yabt li
five more saying: 'Master, you gave me five talents,
ha xammeS xranyan ittagret 'alaihen.
see, five more I have added to them.'
amar leh mareh: ew 'abda Taba wamhaimna
His master said to him: 'Well done, good and faithful servant,
'al qallil mhaiman wait 'al saggi aqqimak
you were faithful over little, over much I will put you in charge,
'ol lxaduteh dmarak.
enter into the joy of your master.'
waqreb haw dtartein kakrawhi wemar: mari tartein
And the one with two talents came up saying: 'Master, two
kakrin yabt li ha tartein xranyan ittagret 'alaihen.
talents you gave me, see, two others I have added to them.'
amar leh mareh: ew 'abdaTaba wamhaimna
His master said to him: 'Well done, good and faithful servant,
'al qallil mhaiman wayt 'al saggi aqqimak
you were faithful over little, over much I will put you in charge,

153

'ol lxaduteh dmarak.
enter into the joy of your master.'
qreb ger ap haw dansab xada kakra wemar:
Then also came up the one who received one talent, saying:
mari yada' weit lak gabra att qaSya
'Master, I knew that you were a harsh man,
wxaced att ayka dla zra't
reaping where you did not sow
wamkanneS att min aika dla badart
and gathering where you did not scatter,
wdexlet wezzet TaSSitah kakrak bar'a:
so I was afraid and I went and hid your talent in the ground.
ha it lak dilak.
Here you have what is yours.'
'ana mareh wemar leh:
His master in reply said to him:
'abda biSa waxbennana:
'You bad and lazy servant.
yada wait dxaced-na aika dla zar'et
You knew that I reap where I did not sow
wamkanneS-na min aika dla badret:
and gather where I did not scatter,
wale wa lak dtarme kespi 'al patora wate weit ana
you should have put my money in the bank, and on my return
wtaba weit dili 'am ribbyateh.
I would have got my own back with interest.
sabu hakel minneh kakra
So take the talent from him
whabuh lhaw dit leh 'asar kakrin.
and give it to the one with ten talents.'
For to one who has, more will be given
wittawsap leh:
and will have an abundance;
haw den dlait leh
but from the one who has not,
wap haw dit leh iSitqel minneh.
even what he has will be taken away.
wal'abda baTTila apquhi lxeSSoka baraya
And this useless servant throw him into the outer darkness.
tamman ihwe bikya wxuraq Sinne.
There will be weeping and gnashing of teeth.

The Last Judgment

Mt25,31-46

ma date den breh dnaSa bSubxeh wkullhon malakawhi
When the Son of man comes in his glory and all his holy angels

qaddiSe 'ammeh haiden itteb 'al tronos dSubxeh.
with him, then he will sit on the throne of his glory.

witkanSun qdamawhi kullhon 'amme waipareS innon
Before him will be gathered all nations, and he will separate them

xad min xad ak ra'ya dampareS 'erbe min gdaiya.
one from another as a shepherd separates the sheep from the goats.

waiqim 'erbe min yammineh wagdaiya min semmaleh.
and he will put the sheep at his right hand and the goats at the left.

haiden yemar malka lhanon dmin yammineh:
Then the King will say to those at his right hand:

taw brikawhi dabi:
'Come, the blessed of my Father,

iratu malkuta da'atida wat lkon
inherit the kingdom prepared for you

min tarmyateh d'alma.
from the foundation of the world.

kipnet ger wyabtun li lmekal wachet waSqitonani
I was hungry and you gave me food, I was thirsty and you gave me drink,

aksnaya weit wkanneStonani 'arTillaya weit wkassitonani
I was a stranger and you took me in, I was naked and you clothed me,

krih weit was'artonani wbeit assire weit wettaiton lwati.
I was ill and you cared for me, I was in prison and you visited me.'

haiden yemrun leh hanon zaddiqe: maran emmati xazainak
Then the righteous will answer him: 'Lord, when did we see you

dakpen att wtarsinak aw dache att waSqinak?
hungry and feed you or thirsty and give you drink?

wemmati xazainak daksnaya att wkanneSnak
When did we see you a stranger and took you in,

aw d'arTillaya att wkassinak?
or naked and clothe you?

wemmati xazainak krih aw beit assire wettain lwatak?
When did we see you sick or in prison and visit you?'

w'ana malka wemar lhon: amen amar-na lkon dakma
And the King will answer them: 'Truly I tell you, just as you

da'abadton lxad min halen axai z'ore li-w 'abadton.
did it to one of the least of these brothers of mine, you did it to me.'

haiden yemar ap lhanon dmin semmaleh:
Then he also will say to those on his left:

zelu lkon menni liTe lnura dal'alam hay damTaiyaba
'Depart from me, you accursed, into the eternal fire prepared

lakelqarca walmalakawhi.
for the devil and his angels.

kipnet ger wla yabton li lmekal
I was hungry and you gave me no food,
wachet wla aqitonani:
I was thirsty and you gave me no drink,
aksnaya weit wla kanneStonani
I was stranger and you did not take me in.
'arTillaya weit wla kassitonani
I was naked and you did not clothe me.
wakriha wet wbeit assire weit wla s'artonani.
I was sick and in prison and you did not visit me.'
haiden ye'non wap hinnon wyemrun:
Then they also will answer saying:
maran emmati xazainak kapna aw cahaya aw aksnaya
'Lord, when was it that we saw you hungry or thirsty or a stranger
aw 'arTillaya aw krih aw beit assire wla SammeSnak?
or naked or sick or in prison, and did not take care of you?'
haiden ye'ne wyemar lhon:
Then he will answer them:
amen amar-na lkon dakma dla 'abadton lxad min halen z'ore
'Truly I tell you, just as you did not do to one of the least of these,
apla li 'abadton.
you did not do it to me.'
wyezun halen ltaSniqa dal'alam
And these will go away into eternal punishment,
wzaddiqe lxaiye dal'alam.
but the righteous into eternal life.

Greeks seek Jesus
J12,23-26
ettat Sa'ta diSttabbax breh dnaSa.
The hour has come for the Son of man to be glorified.
amen amen amar-na lkon dapridta dxiTTta in la napla wmaitta
Truly, truly I tell you, unless a grain wheat falls and dies
bar'a balxodeh paiSa: in den maitta pere saggiye maittya.
in the earth, remains alone; but if it dies, it bears much fruit.
man draxem napSeh yawbdih
Whoever loves his life loses it,
wman dsane napSeh b'alma hana iTTrih lxaiye dal'alam.
and whoever hates his life in this world will keep it for eternal life.
in li naS mSammeS yete batari:
Whoever serves me must follow me,
waika dana itai tamman ihwe ap mSamSani.
and where I am, there also will my servant be.
man dli mSammeS yaqqriwhi aba.
Whoever serves me, the Father will honor him.

156

His hour has come
J12,27-34

haSa napSi ha SgiSa.
Now my soul is troubled.
wmana emar: abi paccani min hade Sa'ta?
And what should I say: Father, save me from this hour?
ella miTTol hana etteit lhade Sa'ta.
But it is for this purpose that I came to this hour.
aba Sabbak Smak.
Father, glorify your name.
la wa miTTolati hawa qala hana ella miTTolatkon.
This voice did not come for my sake but for yours.
haSa dineh-u d'alma hana
Now is the judgment of this world,
haSa arkona d'alma hana miStde lbar.
now the ruler of this world will be driven out.
wana ma dittrimet min ar'a
And I, when I am lifted up from the earth,
egged kollnaS lwati.
I will draw everyone to me.

The light of the world
J12,35-46

qallil xren zabna nuhara 'ammkon-u.
A little while longer the light is among you.
halleku 'ad it lkon nuhara
Walk while you have the light,
dla xeSSoka yadrekkon.
so that darkness may not overcome you.
wman damhallek bxeSSoka la yada' laika azel.
Whoever walks in the dark does not know where he is going.
'ad it lkon nuhara haimenu bnuhara
While you have the light, believe in the light,
dbnawhi dnuhara tihwon.
so that you may become children of light.
man damhaimen bi la wa bi mhaimen ella bman dSaddrani.
Whoever believes in me believes not in me but in him who sent me.
wman dli xaze xaze lman dSaddrani.
And whoever sees me sees him who sent me.
ana nuhara etteyt l'alma dkoll damhaimen bi
I came as light into the world, so that everyone who believes in me
la iqawwe bxeSSoka.
should not remain in the darkness.

157

Judgment by the Word

J12,47-50

wman dSama' millai wla naTar lhen ana la da'en-na leh:
If one hears my words and does not keep them, I do not judge him,
la ger etteit deddun l'alma ella daxxe l'alma.
for I did not come to judge the world but to save the world.
man dTalem li wla mqabbel millai it man dda'en leh:
Whoever rejects me and does not accept my words has a judge:
millta dmallet hi daina leh byawma xraya.
the word that I spoke will judge him on the last day.
dana min napSi la mallet ella aba dSaddrani
For I did not speak on my own but the Father who sent me
hu yab li puqdana mana emar wmana emallel.
he gave me a commandment what to say and what to speak.
wyada'-na dpuqdaneh xaiye innon dal'alam:
And I know that his commandment is eternal life;
ailen hakel dammallel-na aikanna demar li abi
what I speak, therefore, just as my Father told me,
hakanna mmallel-na.
thus I speak.

His death is again predicted

Mt26,1-5 M14,1 L22,1

yad'in atton dbatar trein yawmin hawe picxa
You know that after two days it will be the Passover,
wabreh dnaSa miStlem dizdqep.
and the Son of man will be handed over to be crucified.

Preparation for the Passover

L22,7-14 M14,12 Mt26,18

zelu Taiyebu lan picxa dil'as.
Go and prepare the Passover for us that we may eat it.
ha ma d'alin-tton lamditta paga' bkon gabra
See, when you go into the city, a man will meet you
daSqil graba dmaiya: zelu batreh waika d'a'el.
carrying a jar of water; follow him where he enters.
emmaru lmareh baita: rabban amar aina-w
Say to the owner of the house: 'The teacher says, where is
beit maSirya aika dekol picxa 'am talmidai?
the guest room where I may eat the Passover with my disciples?'
wha hu mxawwe lkon 'illita xada rabta damSawya
He will show you a large upper room that is furnished.
tamman Taiyebu.
there prepare it.

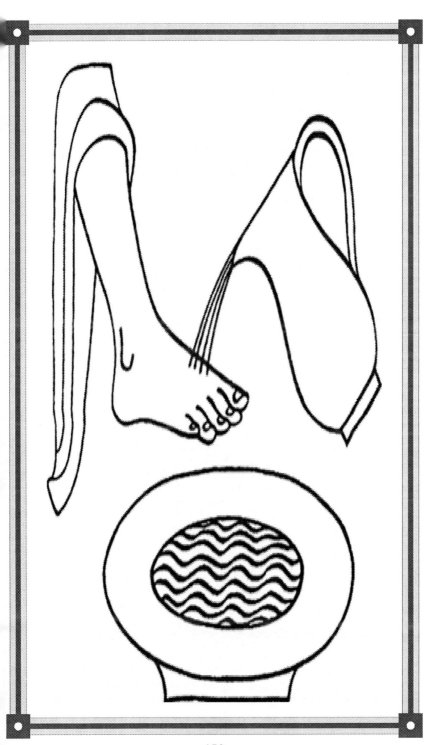

Washing the disciples' feet

J13,7-20

middem d'abed-na att la yada'-att haSa
What I am doing you do not know now,
batarken den tidda'.
but later you will understand.
in la mSig-na lak lait lak 'ammi mnata.
Unless I wash you, you have no share with me.
haw dasxe la sniq ella riglawhi balxod iSig
One who has bathed does not need to wash, except for the feet.
kulleh ger dke-w: ap atton dkaiya atton ella la kullhon.
but is entirely clean; and you are clean, but not all.
yad'in atton mana 'ebdet lkon?
Do you know what I have done to you?
atton qarein-tton li rabban wmaran: Sappir amriton itai ger.
You call me Teacher and Lord - and you are right, for so I am.
in ana hakel markon wrabbkon aSSiget lkon riglaikon
So if I, your Lord and Teacher, have washed your feet,
kma atton xaiyabin-tton datSigun rigle xad dxad.
you also ought to wash one another's feet.
hana ger Tupsa yebbet lkon
For I have given you an example,
daikanna dana 'ebdet lkon ap atton te'bdun.
that as I have done to you, you also should do.
amen amen amar-na lkon dlait 'abda drab min mareh
Truly truly I tell you, a servant is not greater than his master
wla Slixa drab min dSaddreh.
nor a messenger is greater than the one who sent him.
in halen tid'un Tubane atton in te'bdun innen.
If you know these things, you are blessed if you do them.
la wa 'al kullkon amar-na: yada'-na ger lailen dagbet.
I am not speaking of all of you; I know whom I have chosen.
ella daktaba iSlam:
But so that the scripture might be fulfilled:
dhaw dakel 'ammi laxma arim 'alai 'qbeh.
'The one who ate bread with me has lifted his heel against me.'
min haSa amar-na lkon min qdam dihwe
From now on I am telling you before it happens,
dma dahawa thaimnun dana-na.
so that when it happens you may believe that I am he.
amen amen amar-na lkon dman damqabbel
Truly, truly I tell you, whoever receives
lman damSaddar-na li mqabbel:
one whom I send receives me;
wman dli mqabbel mqabbel lman dSaddrani.
and whoever receives me receives him who sent me.

His betrayal predicted

J13,21 M14,18 Mt26,21

amen amen amar-na lkon dxad minnkon yaSilmani.
Truly, truly I tell you, one of you will betray me.
haw-u dcaba'-na laxma wyaheb-na leh.
It is the one for whom I dip the bread and give it to him.
man dcaba' ideh 'ammi blagta hu yaSilmani.
One who dips his hand with me in the dish will betray me.
middem d'abed att 'abed b'agal.
What you are going to do, do it quickly.
wabreh dnaSa azel aikanna daktib 'alawhi:
For the Son of man goes as it is written about him,
wai leh lgabra haw dbideh breh dnaSa miStlem.
but woe to the man by whose hand the Son of man is betrayed.
paqqax wa leh lgabra haw illu la itiled.
It would have been better for that man if he had not been born.
[Judas asked: 'Surely not I, Rabbi?']
att emart.
You have said so.

The Last Supper

L22,15 M14,15 Mt26,26 1Cor11,23

rigta ragtani dhana picxa ekol 'ammkon qdam dexaS:
With desire I desired to eat this Passover with you before I suffer;
amar-na lkon ger dmikkel la ekliwhi
for I tell you, I will not eat it again
'adamma diSlam bmalkuteh dalaha.
until it is fulfilled in the kingdom of God.
sabu hana wpallegu bainatkon: amar-na ger lkon
Take this and divide it among yourselves; for I tell you that
dla eSte min yalda dagpitta
I will not drink of the fruit of the vine
'adamma dtete malkuta dalaha:
until the kingdom of God comes:
'adamma lyawma dbeh eSteyuhi xadta 'ammkon bmalkuteh dabi
until that day when I drink it new with you in my Father's kingdom.
sabu akelu hana-w pagri d'al appaikon mitiheb.
Take, eat it: this is my body, which is given for you.
hade hawaiton 'abdin ldukrani.
Do this in remembrance of me.
hana kasa daqyama xadatta bdemi daxalapaikon miteSed.
This cup is the new covenant in my blood which is shed for you.
sabu eStau minneh kullhon: hana demi daqyama xadatta
take drink of it all of you, for this my blood of the new covenant,
daxalap saggiye miteSed lSubqana daxaTahe.
which is shed for the sake of many for the forgiveness of sins.

161

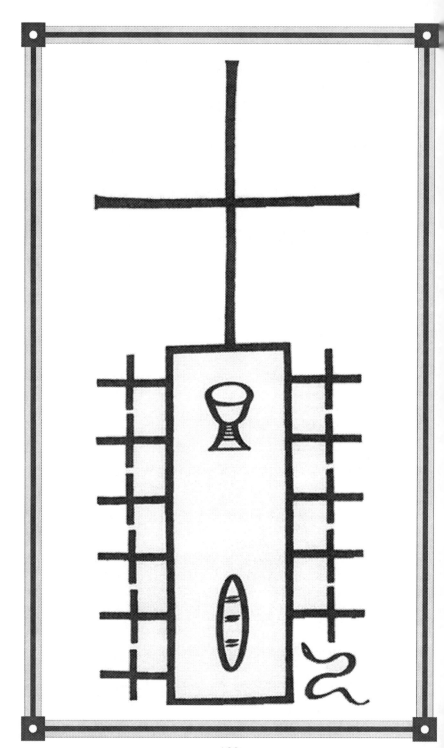

The new commandment of love

J13,31-35

haSa iStabbax breh dnaSa walaha iStabbax beh:
Now is the Son of man glorified and God has been glorified in him.

win alaha iStabbax beh wap alaha mSabbax leh beh
If God is glorified in him, God will also glorify him in himself

wmixda mSabbax leh.
and at once will glorify him.

bnai qallil xren 'ammkon-na.
My children, I am with you only a little longer.

wtib'onani waikanna demret laihudaye:
You will look for me; and as I said to the Jews:

dlaika dana azel-na atton la miSkxin-tton lmeta
'Where I am going you cannot come,'

wap lkon amar-na haSa.
so now I say it to you too.

puqdana xadta yaheb-na lkon dahawaiton maxbin xad lxad
A new commandment I give to you, that you love one another.

aikanna dana axebtkon ap atton taxbun xad lxad.
Just as I have loved you, you also should love one another.`

bhade idda' kollnaS dtalmidai atton
By this everyone will know that you are my disciples,

in xubba ihwe bkon xad lwat xad.
if you have love for one another.

Peter's denial foretold

J13,36 L22,31 Mt26,31

laika dazel-na la miSkax att haSa dtete batari:
Where I go, you cannot follow me now,

lxarta den tete.
but afterward you will follow.

napSak xalapai sa'em att?
Will you lay down your life for me?

amen amen amar-na lak dla iqre tarnagla
Truly, truly I tell you, the cock will not crow

'adamma dtikpor bi tlat zabnin.
before you deny me three times.

ha saTana Sa'el dye'robkon ak dalxiTTe
Look, Satan demanded to sift you like wheat

wana b'et 'alaik dla texsar haimanutak:
but I have prayed for you that your faith may not fail;

wap att bazban itpanni
and you, when once you have turned back,

wSarrar axaik.
strengthen your brothers.

163

The two swords

L22,31-38 Mt26,30 M14,26

atton kullkon titkaSlun bi bhana lilya lilya ktib ger:
All of you will be offended by me in this night, for it is written:
demxe Ira'ya witbadrun 'erbe d'aneh.
'I will strike the shepherd and the sheep of the flock will scatter.'
min batar dqa'em-na den qadem-na Ikon laglila.
But after I have been raised, I will go ahead of you to Galilee.
kad Saddartkon dla kise wadla tarmale wamsane
When I sent you out without a purse, bag or sandals,
Ima xasar Ikon middem?
did you lack anything?
min haSa man dit leh kisa issab whakanna ap tarmala.
But now the one who has a purse should take it and likewise a bag.
wman dlait leh saipa izabben naxteh wizbben leh saipa.
And the one who has no sword should sell his cloak and buy one.
amar-na Ikon ger dap hade daktiba wale dtitmalle bi:
For I tell you, also this scripture must be fulfilled in me:
'am 'awwle itmne.
'He was counted among the wicked.'
kullhon ger da'alai iStallam.
Indeed, everything about me has its fulfillment.
sapqin.
It is enough.

I am the Way

J14,1-14

la itdawad libbkon: haimenu balaha wbi haimenu.
Let not your hearts be troubled; believe in God, believe also in me.
saggiyin innon awwane beit abi:
There are many abodes in my Father's house;
win la amar weit Ikon dazel-na deTaiyeb Ikon atra?
if not so, would I have told you that I go to prepare place for you?
win ezal eTaiyeb Ikon atra tub ete
And if I go and prepare a place for you, I will come again
witbarkon lwati daika dana itay wap atton tihwon.
and take you to myself, so that where I am you also may be.
wlaika dazel-na yad'in-tton wurxa yad'in-tton.
And where I am going you know and the way you know.
ana-na urxa waSrara wxaiye:
I am the way, and the truth, and the life;
la naS ate lwat abi ella in bi.
No one comes to my Father except through me.
illu li yad'in waiton ap labi yad'in waiton:
If you had known me, you would have known my Father also;

164

wmin haSa yad'in-tton leh waxazaitonahi.
from now on you know him and have seen him.
hana kulleh zabna 'ammkon-na wla yada'tani pilippa?
All this time I have been with you and you do not know me, Philip?
man dli xaze xaza laba.
Whoever has seen me has seen the Father.
waikanna att amar att: xawwan aba?
How come you are saying: 'Show us Father'?
la mhaimen att dana babi wabi bi?
Do you not believe that I am in the Father and the Father is in me?
wmille ailen dana mmallel-na min napSi la mmallel-na:
And those words that I speak, on my own I do not speak,
abi den dbi 'amar hu 'abed 'abade halen.
but my Father who dwells in me is doing these works.
haimenu dana babi wabi bi:
Believe that I am in the Father and the Father is in me;
win la apin miTTol 'abade haimenu.
if you do not, then believe because of the works.
amen amen amar-na lkon dman damhaimen bi
Truly, truly I tell you, that the one who believes in me,
'abade ailen dana 'abed ap hu ye'bbed
those works that I do, he will also do.
wadyattirin min halen ye'bbed:
and greater ones than these he will do,
dana lwat aba azel-na.
because I am going to the Father.
wmiddem dtiSilun bSemi e'bbed lkon
Whatever you ask in my name, I will do it for you,
diStabbax aba babreh.
so that the Father may be glorified in the Son.
win tiSilunani bSemi ana 'abed-na.
If you ask anything in my name, I will do it.

The promise of the Paraclyte
J14,15-26

in raxmin-tton li puqdanai Taru.
If you love me, you keep my commandments.
wana eb'e min abi waxrena paraqleTa itten lkon
And I will ask the Father, and another Helper he will give you
dihwe 'ammkon l'alam ruxa daSrara
to be with you forever, the Spirit of truth,
haw d'alma la miSkax lamqabbaluteh
whom the world cannot receive,
dla xazaihi wla yad'eh.
because it does not see him nor knows him.

atton den yad'in-tton leh dalwatkon 'amar wabkon-u.
But you know him, because he dwells with you and will be in you.

la Sabeq-na lkon yatme: ate-na ger lwatkon.
I will not leave you orphans: I am coming to you.

qallil xren w'alma la xaze li:
In a little while the world will no longer see me,

atton den texzonani.
but you will see me.

dana xai ap atton tixxon.
Because I live, you also will live.

bhaw yawma tid'un dana babi
On that day you will know that I am in my Father,

watton bi wana bkon-na.
and you in me, and I in you.

man dit lwateh puqdanai wnaTar lhon
Whoever has my commandments and keeps them

haw-u maxxeb li:
is the one who loves me.

haw den draxem li itraxem min abi
and whoever loves me will be loved by my Father

wana irxmiwhi wexawweuhi napSi.
and I will love him and reveal myself to him.

man draxem li millati naTar:
Whoever loves me keeps my word,

wabi irxmiwhi walwateh atein nan
and my Father will love him, and we will come to him

wawwana lwateh 'abdin nan.
and make our abode with him.

haw den dla raxem li millati la naTar:
Whoever does not love me does not keep my words;

wmillta hade dSam'in-tton la wat dili
and this word that you hear is not mine,

ella daba dSaddrani.
but is the Father's who sent me.

halen mallet 'ammkon kad lwatkon itai.
I have said these things to you while I am still with you.

hu den paraqleTa ruxa dqudSa
But the Helper, the Holy Spirit,

haw damSaddar abi bSemi
whom my Father will send in my name

hu yallepkon kollmiddem.
will teach you everything,

whu i'ahedkon koll ma damar-na lkon.
and remind you of all that have said to you.

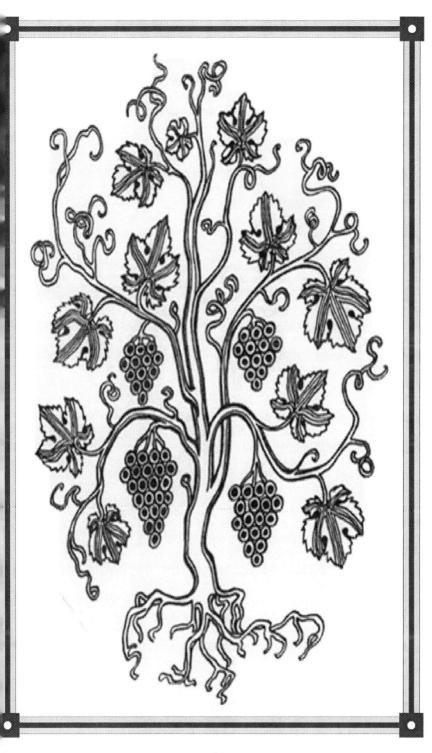

The gift of peace

J14,27-31

Slama Sabeq-na lkon Slama dili yaheb-na lkon:
Peace I leave to you, my peace I give to you;
la wa akanna dyaheb 'alma ana yaheb-na lkon.
not as the world gives do I give it to you.
la itdawad blibbkon wla idxal.
Do not let your hearts be troubled or be afraid.
Sma'ton dana emret lkon: dazel-na wate-na lwatkon.
You heard me to tell you: I am going away and I am coming to you.
illu raxmin waiton li xadein waiton dazel-na lwat abi
If you loved me, you would rejoice that I am going to my Father,
dabi rab-u menni:
because my Father is greater than me.
whaSa ha emret lkon 'adla ihwe
And now I have told you this before it happens,
dma dahawa thaimnun.
so that when it happens you may believe.
mikkel la emallel 'ammkon saggiyata
I will no longer speak much with you,
ate ger arkoneh d'alma.
for the ruler of the world is coming.
wbi lait leh middem ella dida' 'alma
And in me he has nothing, but so that the world may know
draxem-na labi waikanna dpaqdani abi hakwat 'abed-na.
that I love my Father and I do just as my Father commanded me.
qumu nezal mikka.
Get up, let us depart from here.

The true Vine

J15,1-8

ana-na gpitta daSrara wabi-w pallaxa.
I am the true vine, and my Father is the vine grower.
koll SbiSta dbi pere la yabba Saqel lah
Every branch in me that bears no fruit he takes it away,
waida dyabba pere mdakke lah dpere saggiye taitte.
Every branch that bears fruit he prunes that it may bear more fruit.
atton min kaddu dkein-tton miTTol millta dmallet 'ammkon.
You are already pruned by the word that I have spoken to you.
qawwau bi wana bkon.
Remain in me and I in you.
aikanna daSbiSta la miSkxa dtitten pere min napSah in la
Just as the branch cannot yield fruit by itself unless
mqawwya bagpitta hakanna apla atton in la tqawwon bi.
it remains in the vine, neither can you unless you remain in me.

168

ana-na gpitta watton SbiSte:
I am the vine, you are the branches.
man damqawwe bi wana beh hana maitte pere saggiye:
Whoever remains in me and I in him bears much fruit,
miTTol dadla ana la miSkxin-tton lme'bbad middem.
because apart from me you can do nothing.
in la den naS mqawwe bi miSde lbar ak SbiSta
Whoever does not remain in me is thrown away like a branch
dyabSa wlaqTin ramen lah bnura dteqad.
that withers; they pluck it and throw it into the fire to burn.
in den tqawwon bi wmillai tqawwyan bkon
If you remain in me and my words remain in you,
koll ma dticbun lmiSal ihwe lkon.
whatever you wish to ask will be done for you.
bhade miStabbax aba dpere saggiye taiton
By this the Father is glorified, that you bear much fruit,
wtihwon talmidai.
and become my disciples.

Remain in my love
J15,9-17
aikanna daxbani abi ap ana axebtkon:
As my Father has loved me, so I have loved you;
qawwau brixmati dili.
remain in my love.
in puqdanai tiTTrun tqawwon bxubba dili
If you keep my commandments, you will remain in my love,
aikanna dana niTret puqdanawhi dabi wamqawwe-na bxubbeh
as I have kept my Father's commandments and remain in his love.
halen mallet 'ammkon dxadwati tihwe bkon
These things I have spoken to you that my joy may be in you
wtiStamle xadwatkon.
and that your joy may be complete.
hana-w puqdani dtaxbun xad lxad
This is my commandment, that you love one another
aikanna dana axebtkon.
as I have loved you.
xubba drab min hana lait dnaS napSeh isim
No one has greater love than this, to lay down one's life
xalap raxmanawhi.
for one's friends.
atton raxmai atton in te'bdun koll dampaqqed-na lkon.
You are my friends if you do what I command you.
la mikkel qare-na lkon 'abde
No longer do I call you servants,

169

miTTol d'abda la yada' mana 'abed mareh:
because a servant does not know what his master is doing;
raxmai den qreitkon miTTol dkoll dSim'et
but I have called you friends, because everything that I heard
min abi awda'tkon.
from my Father I made known to you.
la wa atton gbaitonani ella ana-w gbeitkon wsamtkon
You did not choose me but I chose you and appointed you
dap atton tezun taitton pere wperaikon iqawwon.
to go and bear fruit, and that your fruit may remain,
dkoll dtiSalun lab bSemi itten lkon.
so that whatever you ask the Father in my name he may give you
halen mpaqqed-na lkon dtaxxbun xad lxad.
This I command you that you love one another.

The world's hatred

J15, 18-25

win 'alma sane lkon da'u daqdamikon li sna.
If the world hates you, know that it hated me before you.
willu min 'alma waiton 'alma ldileh raxem-wa:
If you were of the world, the world would love its own;
ella la hawaiton min 'alma: ana ger gbetkon min 'alma
but you are not of the world, for I chose you out of the world,
miTTol hana sane lkon 'alma.
therefore the world hates you.
'ahadu millta dana emret lkon:
Remember the word that I said to you:
dlait 'abda drab min mareh.
A servant is not greater than his master.
in li rdapu ap lkon irdepun:
If they persecuted me, they will persecute you;
win millati nTaru ap dilkon iTTrun.
if they kept my word, they will keep yours also.
ella halen kullhen ye'bbdun bkon miTTol Semi
But they will do all these things on account of my name,
dla yad'in dman dSaddrani.
because they do not know him who sent me.
illu ana la etteit mallet 'ammhon lait wat lhon xaTita:
If I had not come and spoken to them, they would not have sin,
haSa den lait lhon 'ilta 'al appai xaTahaihon.
but now they have no excuse for their sin.
man dli sane ap labi sane.
Whoever hates me hates my Father also.
willu 'abade la 'ibdet l'enaihon ailen dnaS xren la 'abad
If I had not done among them the works that no one else did,

lait wat lhon xaTita:
they would not have sin.
haSa den waxzau wasnau ap li wap labi:
But now they have seen and hated both me and my Father.
dtitmalle millta daktiba bnamoshon:
It was to fulfill the word that is written in their law:
dasnauni maggan.
'They hated me without a cause.'
ma den detta paraqleTa haw dana mSaddar-na lkon
When the Helper comes, whom I will send to you
min lwat abi ruxa daSrara haw dmin lwat abi napeq
from my Father, the Spirit of truth who proceeds from the Father,
hu ished 'alai: ap atton sahadin-tton
he will testify on my behalf. You also testify
dmin Suraya 'ammi atton.
because from the beginning you have been with me.

On persecutions
J16,1-4

halen mallet 'ammkon dla titkaSlun.
I have said these things to you that you may not fall away.
yapqunakon ger min knuSthon wtete Sa'ta
They will expel you from the synagogues; and the hour is coming
dkoll diqTolkon isbar dqurbana mqarreb lalaha.
when everyone who kills you will think he is offering service to God.
whalen ye'bbdun miTTol dla ida'u wla abi wla li.
And they will do this because they have not known my Father or me.
halen mallet 'ammkon dma detta 'iddanhen
I have told you this so that when their hour comes
te'hdun innen dana emret lkon.
you may remember that I told you.
halen den min qdim la emret lkon d'ammkon weit.
I did not tell you this from the beginning, because I was with you.

The Holy Spirit promised
J16,5-15

haSa den azel-na li lwat man dSaddrani
But now I am going to him who sent me;
wla naS minnkon mSa'el li: laika azel att?
yet none of you asks me: Where are you going?
emret lkon ger halen wettat karyuta wamlat libbawatkon.
But because I told you this, sorrow came and has filled your hearts.
ella ana Srara amar-na lkon dpaqqax lkon dana ezal:
But I tell you the truth, it is better for you that I go;

171

in den ana la azel-na paraqleTa la ate lwatkon.
If I do not go away, the Helper will not come to you.
in den ezal eSaddriwhi lwatkon.
But if I go, I will send him to you.
wma detta hu yaksiwhi l'alma 'al xaTita
And when he comes, he will convict the world of sin
w'al zaddiquta w'al dina:
and of justice and of judgment:
'al xaTita dla haimnin bi:
of sin, because they do not believe in me;
'al zaddiquta den dalwat abi azel-na
of justice, because I am going to the Father
wla tub xazein-tton li:
and you will see me no longer;
'al dina den darkona d'alma hana din-u.
of judgment, because the ruler of this world has been judged.
tub saggi it li lmemar lkon ella la miSkxin-tton lmexad haSa.
I have much more to tell you, but you cannot bear it now.
ma detta den ruxa daSrara hu idabbarkon bkulleh Srara:
When the Spirit of truth comes, he will guide you into all the truth,
la ger imallel min re'yan napSeh ella koll diSma'
for he will not speak on his own, but whatever he hears
haw imallel w'atidata yawdda'akon.
he will speak and will declare what is to come.
whu iSabbxani miTTol dmin dili yasseb
He will glorify me, because he will take from what is mine
waixawweikon.
and declare it to you.
kollmiddem dit labi dili-w.
Everything that my Father has is mine.
miTTol hana emret lkon dmin dili yasseb
For this reason I told you that he will take from what is mine
waixawweikon.
and will declare it to you.

Sorrow turned to joy

J16,16-22

qallil wla texzonani wtub qallil
A little while, and you will no longer see me, and again a little while
wtexzonani dazel-na lwat aba.
and you will see me, because I go to the Father.
'al hade ba'ein-tton 'am xadade demret lkon:
Is this what you are asking among yourselves, because I said:
dqallil wla texzonani wtub qallil wtexzonani?
A little while and you will not see me and again a little and you will see me?

172

amen amen amar-na lkon dtibkon atton wtelon
Truly, truly I tell you, you will weep and mourn,
w'alma ixde walkon tikre:
but the world will rejoice and you will have pain,
ella karyutkon lxaduta tihwe.
but your pain will turn into joy.
attta ma dyalda karya lah
When a woman is in labor, she has pain,
damTa yawma dmawladah:
because the day of her delivery has come,
ma dildat den bra la 'ahda ulcana
but when her child is born, she no longer remembers the anguish
miTTol xaduta ditiled barnaSa b'alma.
because of the joy that a child has been born into the world.
ap atton haSa karya lkon
So you have pain now,
tub den exzeikon wixde libbkon
but I will see you again, and your hearts will rejoice
wxaddutkon la naS yasseb minnkon.
and no one will take your joy from you.

Prayer in his name
J16,23-28
wabhaw yawma li la tiSalun middem:
On that day you will ask nothing of me.
amen amen amar-na lkon:
Truly, truly I tell you,
dkoll middem dtiSalun labi bSemi itten lkon.
if you ask anything of my Father in my name, he will give it to you.
'adamma lhaSa la Selton middem bSemi.
Until now you have not asked anything in my name.
Salu wtisbun dtihwe xaddutkon mSamlya.
Ask and you will receive, so that your joy may be complete.
halen bpillata mallet 'ammkon:
I have said these things to you in proverbs.
atya den Sa'ta emmati dla emallel 'ammkon bpillata
The hour is coming when I will no longer speak to you in proverbs
ella 'eyn bagle ebaddeq lkon 'al aba.
but I will tell you plainly about the Father.
bhaw yawma dtiSalun bSemi:
On that day you will ask in my name,
wla amar-na lkon dana eb'e min aba 'alaikon:
I do not say to you that I will ask the Father for you;
hu ger aba raxem lkon datton rxemtonani
for the Father himself loves you, because you have loved me

173

whaimenton dana min lwat aba nipqet.
and have believed that I came from the Father.
nipqet min lwat aba wetteit l'alma
I came from the Father and have come into the world,
wtub Sabeq-na l'alma wazel-na li lwat aba:
and again I am leaving the world and am going to the Father.
haimenu? dha atya Sa'ta whaSa ettat
Do you believe? Behold, the hour is coming, and now has come,
dtitbaddrun naS latreh
when you will be scattered each to his home
wtiSbqunani balxodai.
and leave me alone.
wla haweit balxodai daba 'ammi-u.
Yet I am not alone because the Father is with me.
halen emret lkon dbi ihwe lkon Slama.
I have said this to you, so that in me you may have peace.
b'alma hawe lkon ulcana.
In the world you have tribulation.
ella itlabbabu: ana zkeiteh l'alma.
But take courage! I have conquered the world.

THE PRAYER OF THE HIGH PRIEST

The Prayer for Himself

J17,1-5

abi ettat Sa'ta:
Father, the hour has come,
Sabbax brak dabrak iSabbxak
glorify your Son so that the Son may glorify you
aikanna dyabt leh SulTana 'al koll bsar
just as you gave him power over all flesh,
dkoll ma dyabt leh itten leh xaiye dal'alam.
so that he may give eternal life to all you gave him.
halen innen den xaiye dal'alam did'unak datt
And this is eternal life, that they may know you,
alaha dSrara balxodaik wman dSaddart yeSu' mSixa.
the only true God, and whom you sent, Jesus the Messiah.
ana Sabbaxtak b'ara:
I glorified you on earth:
'abada haw dyabt li de'bbed Sallemteh.
the work that you gave me to do I have finished.
whaSa Sabbaxani att abi lwatak bhaw Subxa
So now, Father, glorify me with yourself with the glory
dit wa li lwatak min qdam dihwe 'alma.
that I had with you before the world existed.

174

The Prayer for the disciples

J17,6-19

awdd'et Smak IbnainaSa hanon dyabt li min 'alma:
I revealed your name to men whom you gave me from the world.
dilak wau wli yabt innon
They were yours and you gave them to me
wanTaru milltak.
and they have kept your word.
haSa yed'et dkoll ma dyabt li min lwatak-u:
Now they know that everything you gave me is from you;
dmille yabt li yebbet lhon
for the words that you gave to me I have given to them,
whinnon qabbelu wida'u Sarrira'it dmin lwatak napqet
and they accepted them and truly understood that I came from you,
whaimenu datt Saddartani.
and they have believed that you sent me.
wana 'alaihon ba'e-na: la wa 'al 'alma ba'e-na
And I am praying for them; for the world I am not praying,
ella 'al hanon dyabt li ddilak innon.
but for those you have given me, because they are yours.
wkoll middem ddili-w dilak-u wdilak dili-w:
And everything that is mine is yours and yours is mine;
wamSabbax-na bhon.
and I have been glorified in them.
wmikkel la haweit b'alma whalen b'alma innon
And now I am no longer in the world, but they are in the world.
wana lwatak ate-na.
and I am coming to you.
aba qaddiSa: Tar innon baSmak haw dyabt li
Holy Father, protect them in your name that you have given me,
dihwon xad aikanna daxanan.
so that they may be one, just as we are.
kad 'ammhon weit b'alma ana naTar weit lhon baSmak
When I was with them I protected them in your name
wlailen dyabt li niTret:
that you have given me and I guarded them;
wnaS minnhon la ebbad ella breh dabdana
and not one of them was lost except the son of perdition,
ditmalle ktaba.
so that the scripture might be fulfilled.
haSa den lawatak ate-na whalen mmallel-na b'alma
But now I am coming to you, and I speak this in the world
dtihwe xadwati mSamlya bhon.
so that they may have my joy made complete in themselves.

175

ana yebbet lhon milltak w'alma sna innon,
I have given them your word, and the world hated them,
dla wa min 'alma aikanna dana la weit min 'alma.
because they are not of the world, just as I am not of the world.
la wa dtiSqol innon min 'alma ba'e-na
Not to take them out of the world I am asking you,
ella dtiTTar innon min biSa.
but to protect them from the Evil.
la wau ger min 'alma aikanna dana la weit min 'alma.
They are not of the world, just as I am not of the world.
aba qaddeS innon baSrarak dmilltak dilak Srara-y.
Father, sanctify them in the truth, for your word is truth.
aikanna dli Saddart l'alma ap ana Saddret innon l'alma.
As you sent me into the world, so I sent them into the world.
w'al appaihon ana mqaddeS-na napSi
And I consecrate myself for them,
dihwon ap hinnon mqaddSin baSrara.
so that they also may be consecrated in truth.

The Prayer for the Church
J17,20-26

wla 'al appai halen ba'e-na balxod
I pray not only for them,
ella ap 'al appai ailen damhaimnin bi bmillathon
but also for those who will believe in me through their word,
dkullhon ihwon xad aikanna datt abi bi wana bak:
that they may all be one, as you, Father, are in me and I in you,
dap hinnon ban xad ihwon:
that they also may be one in us,
dayhaimen 'alma datt Saddartani.
so that the world may believe that you sent me.
wana Subxa dyabt li yebbet lhon
The glory that you have given me I have given them,
dihwon xad aikanna daxanan xad xanan.
that they be one, as we are one.
ana bhon watt bi dihwon gmirin lxad
I in them and you in me, that they may become perfectly one,
wadidda' 'alma datt Saddartani.
so that the world may know that you have sent me
wdaxabet innon aikanna dap li axxebt.
and have loved them even as you have loved me.
aba hanon dyabt li cabe-na dattar dana ap hinnon ihwon.
Father, I wish that those you gave me may be also where I am
'ammi dihwon xazein Subxa dili haw dyabt li:
with me, so that they may see my glory that you gave me,

daxxebtani min qdam tarmyateh d'alma.
because you loved me before the foundation of the world.
abi zaddiqa: w'alma la yad'ak
Righteous Father, the world does not know you,
ana den ida'tak whinnon ida'u datt Saddartani.
but I know you; and these know that you have sent me.
wawdd'et innon Smak wmawdda'-na
And I made known to them your name and I will make it known.
dxubba haw daxxebtani
so that the love with which you loved me
ihwe bhon wana ehwe bhon.
may be in them, and I may be in them.

Gethsemane
                              Mt26,36-46 M14,32-42 L22,39-46
tebu harka 'ad ezal ecalle.
Sit down here while I go and pray.
karya-y lah InapSi 'adamma Imawta
I feel sadness in my soul even to death.
qawwau li harka waSharru 'ammi.
Wait for me here and keep awake with me.
aba kol middem miSkax att:
Father, all things are possible to you.
a'bar menni kasa hana:
Take this cup away from me;
bram la ak dana cabe-na ella ak datt.
but not as I want, but as you do.
Sim'on dmikt lak? la iSkaxet xada Sa'a Imitt'aru?
Simon,are you asleep? Could you not keep awake one hour?
hakanna la iSkaxton xada Sa'a dtiSihron 'ammi?
So you were not able to be awake with me for one hour?
itt'iru wcallau dla te''alun Inisyona.
keep awake and pray that you may not enter into temptation.
ruxa mTayyeba pagra den krih.
The spirit is willing but the flesh is weak.
abi in la miSkax hana kasa dye'bar
Father, if it is not possible for this cup to pass
ella in eStiteh ihwe cibyanak.
but I must drink it, your will be done.
dmaku mikkel wittnixu ha mTat Sa'ta
Sleep from now on and rest, behold the hour has arrived
wabreh dnaSa miStlem bidaihon dxaTTaye.
and the Son of man is betrayed into the hands of sinners.
qumu nezal: ha mTa haw dmaSlem li.
Get up, let us be going! See, at hand is the one who betrays me!

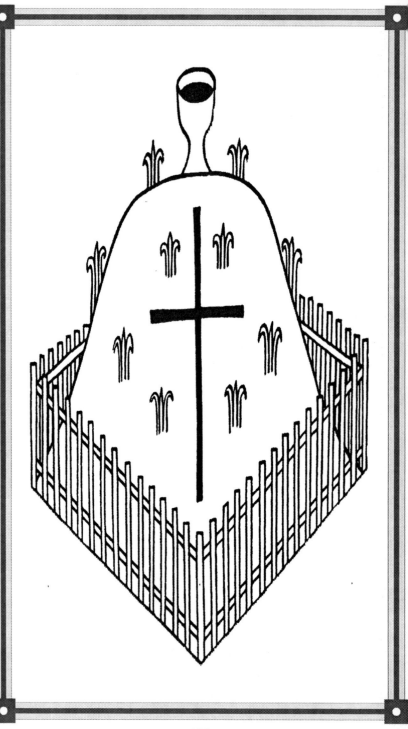

Betrayal and arrest

Mt26,47 M14,43 L22,47 J18,2

'al hai dettait xaberi?
About this that you have come, my friend?
ihuda bnuSiqta maSlem att leh labreh dnaSa?
Judas, with the kiss you are betraying the Son of man?
Iman ba'ein-tton?
Whom are you looking for?
ana-na: Iman ba'ein-tton?
I am he. Whom are you looking for?
emret Ikon dana-na:
I told you that I am he.
win li ba'ein-tton Sboqu lhalen azin.
If you are looking for me, then let these men go.
sim sapsera bxiltah!
Put your sword back into its sheath!
kasa dyab li abi la eStewhi?
The cup that my Father gave me shall I not drink?
kaddu 'adamma lhade!
No more of this!
ahppeq sapsera Idukkta:
Put your sword back into its place,
kullhon den hanon dansabu saipe
for all who take the sword
bsaype imutun.
will perish by the sword.
aw sabar att dla miSkax-na deb'e min abi
Or do you think that I cannot ask of my Father
waiqim li haSa yattir min tart'esre ligyonin dmalake?
and he will raise me at once more than twelve legions of angels?
aikanna hakel itmallon ktabe dhakanna wale dihwe?
How then may the scriptures be fulfilled that it must be so?
ak d'al gaiyasa ipaqton bsapsare wabxuTre
As against a robber you came out with swords and clubs
dtexdunani?
to capture me?
kullyom Iwatkon bhaikla yateb wmallep
Every day I sat among you in the temple teaching
wla exadtonani:
and you did not arrest me.
hade den dahawat ditmallon ktabe danbiyye:
This happened that the scriptures of the prophets may be fulfilled.
ella hada-y Sa'atkon wSulTana dxeSSoka:
But this is your hour, and the power of darkness.

179

Before the Sanhedrin

J18,13-24 Mt26,57-67 L22,54-70 M14,53-64

ana 'ein bagle mallet 'am 'amma:
I have spoken openly among the people;
wabkollzban allepet baknuSta wabhaikla
I have always taught in synagogues and in the temple,
aika dkullhon yudaye mitkanSin
where all the Jews come together;
wmiddem bTuSya la mallet.
I have said nothing in secret.
mana mSa'el att li?
Why do you ask me?
Sa'el lhanon daSma'u mana mallet 'ammhon:
Ask those who heard what I said to them;
ha hinnon yad'in koll middem demret.
look, they know what I said.
[To an officer who struck him]
in biSa'it mallet ashed 'al biSa
I have spoken wrongly, testify to the wrong;
win den Sappir Imana mxaittani?
but if rightly, why do you strike me?
[Kaiphas: 'Tell us if you are the Messiah, the Son of God.']
att emart.
You have said so.
[Chief priests and scribes: 'If you are the Messiah, tell us.']
in emar Ikon la thaimnunani
If I tell you, you will not believe me,
win eSa'elkon la mpannein-tton li pitgama aw Sarein-tton li.
and if I question you, you will not answer me nor release me.
amar-na Ikon den dmin haSa tixzonani
But I tell you that from now on you will see
labreh dnaSa dyateb min yammina dxaila dalaha
the Son of man sitting at the right hand of Power of God
wate 'al 'ananai Smaiya.
and coming on the clouds of heaven.
[Chief priests and scribes: 'Are you the Son of God, then?']
atton amrin-tton dana-na:
You say yourselves that I am.

Before Pilate - I am a King

J18,29-37 Mt27,11-14

[Pilate asked: 'Are you king of the Jews?']
min napSak emart hade aw xrane emaru lak 'alai?
Do you say this on your own or have others told you about me?
malkuta dili la hawat min hana 'alma.
My kingdom is not from this world.

malkuta dili la hawat min hana 'alma.
My kingdom is not from this world.
illu min 'alma wat hana malkuti mitkatSin waw mSamSanai
If my kingdom were from this world, my servants would fight
dla iStlem layudaye:
that I would not be handed over to the Jews.
haSa den malkuti dili la wat mikka.
But now my kingdom is not from here.
[Pilate asked him: 'So you are a king?']
att emart dmalka-na.
You say that I am a king.
ana lhade ilid-na walhade etteit l'alma.
For this I was born and for this I came into the world.
koll man ditawhi min Srara Sama' qali.
Everyone who is of the truth listens to my voice.
lait wa lak 'alai SulTana
You would have no power over me
apla xad illu ihib wa lak min l'el:
unless it had been given you from above;
miTTol hana haw man daSilmani lak
therefore the one who handed me over to you
rabba-y xaTiteh min dilak.
has the greater sin than you.

VIA DOLOROSA   *To the Daughters of Jerusalem*
L23,28-31

bnat oriSlem la tibkyan 'alay:
Daughters of Jerusalem, do not weep for me,
bram 'al napSkein bkayein w'al bnaikein.
but weep for yourselves and for your children.
dha attein yawmata dabhon yemrun:
For indeed, the days are coming when they will say:
Tubaihen l'ukrata walkarsata dla iled
'Blessed are the barren, and the wombs that never bore
wlatdayya dla ainequ.
and the breasts that never nursed.'
haiden tSarron lmemar lTure: dpelu 'alain!
Then they will begin to say to the mountains: 'Fall on us!'
walramata dkassayeynan:
and to the hills: 'Cover us!'
din bqaisa raTTiba halen 'abdin
For if they do this when the wood is green,
byabbiSa mana ihwe?
when it is dry what will happen?

181

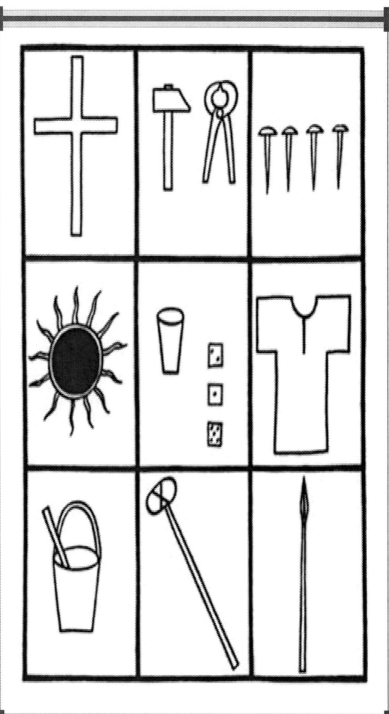

THE SEVEN WORDS ON THE CROSS

First Word

L23,34

aba Sboq lhon la ger yad'in mana 'abdin:
Father, forgive them, for they do not know what they are doing.

Second Word

L23,43

amen amar-na lak dyawmana 'ammi tihwe bpardaisa:
Truly I tell you, today you will be with me in Paradise.

Third Word

J19,26-27

attta ha breki!
Woman, here is your son!
ha immak!
Here is your mother!

Fourth Word

Mt27,46 M15,34

eli eli lmana Sbaqtani?
My God, my God, why have you forsaken me?

Fifth Word

J18,28

che-na!
I thirst!

Sixth Word

J19,30

ha mSallam
Behold, it is finished.

Seventh Word

L23,46

abi bidaik sa'em-na ruxi!
Father, into your hands I commit my spirit!

APPEARANCES AFTER THE RESURRECTION

The appearance to Mary Magdalene
J20,14-18

attta mana bakya atti walman ba'ya atti?
Woman, why are you crying? Whom are you looking for?
maryam! la titqarbin li:
Mary! ... Do not hold on to me,
la ger 'adakkel silqet lwat abi.
because I have not yet ascended to my Father.
zeli den lwat axay wemmari lhon:
But go to my brothers and say to them:
saleq-na lwat abi wabukon walahi walahakon.
'I ascend to my Father and your Father, to my God and your God.'

The appearance to the women
Mt28,9-10

Slam lken!
Peace be to you!
la tidixlan ella zallein emamarein laxai dyezun laglila:
Do not be afraid but go and tell my brothers to go to Galilee;
wtamman yexzonani.
and there they will see me.

On the way to Emmaus - To two disciples
L24,13-35

mana innen mille halen
What are these words
dammallein-tton xad 'am xad
which you are discussing with each other
kad mhallkin-tton wakmirin-tton?
as you walk along looking sad?
[Cleopas asked: 'You do not know the things that happened?']
mana?
What things?
o xassirai re'yana wyaqqirai libba lamhaimanu
Oh, how foolish you are, and how slow of heart to believe
bkullhon aylen dmallelu nbiyye!
all that the prophets spoke!
la wa halen 'atid wa daisaibbar mSixa
Was it not necessary that the Messiah should suffer these things
wadye'ol ItiSboxteh?
and enter into his glory?

184

The appearance to his disciples

L24,36-43 J20,19-23

Slama 'ammkon!
Peace be with you!
mana mitti'zin-tton
Why are you frightened
wmana salqan maxSbata 'al libbwatkon?
and why questions arise in your hearts?
xazau idai wriglai dana-na
See my hands and my feet that it is I myself,
goSSunani wda'u:
touch me and see,
dalruxa bisra wgarme lait lah
for a spirit does not have flesh and bones
ak dxazeiton dit li:
as you see that I have.
it Ikon middem tnan Imekal?
Have you anything here to eat?

The appearance to Thomas present

J20,26-29

Slama 'ammkon!
Peace be with you!
aitta cib'ak Iharka waxazi idai:
Put your finger here and see my hands;
waitta idak wawSeT bgabbi:
and put out your hand and place it in my side:
wla tihwe la mhaimna ella mhaimna.
and do not be unbelieving but a believer.
haSa daxazaitani haiment?
Now, as you have seen me, you believed?
Tubaihon lailen dla xazauni whaimenu.
Blessed are those who do not see me and believe.

The appearance to the eleven

M16,14-16 J20,21-23

zelu l'alma wakrezu sbarti bkullah brita!
Go into all the world and preach my gospel to the whole creation!
aina damhaimen w'amed xaiye:
Whoever believes and is baptized will be saved;
waina dla mhaimen mixaiyab.
whoever does not believe will be condemned.
atwata den lailen damhaimnin halen iqqpan:
These signs will accompany those who believe:
bSemi Sede yappqun wabliSSane xadte imallun
in my name they will drive out demons, speak in new tongues,
waxawawata iSqlun win samma dmawta iSton
they will pick up serpents and if they drink any deadly thing,
la yahhar innon widaihon isimun 'al krihe
it will not hurt them; they will lay their hands on the sick,
witxalmun.
and they will recover.
Slama 'ammkon!
Peace be with you!
aikanna dSaddrani abi ap ana mSaddar-na Ikon:
As my Father has sent me, so I send you.
qabbelu ruxa dqudSa:
Receive the Holy Spirit.
in tibSqun xaTahe lnaS iStabqun leh:
If you forgive the sins of anyone, they are forgiven him;
win texdun dnaS axidin.
if you retain the sins of any, they are retained.

The appearance in Galilee

Mt28,16-20 M16,14

itiheb li koll SulTan baSmaiya wbar'a:
All power has been given to me in heaven and on earth.
aikanna dSaddrani abi ap ana mSaddar-na Ikon:
as my Father sent me, so also I am sending you.
zelu hakel talmedu kullhon 'amme wa'medu innon
Go therefore and make disciples all nations and baptize them
bSem aba wabra wruxa dqudSa.
in the name of the Father and the Son and the Holy Spirit.
wallepu innon diTTrun kollma dpaqedkon
And teach them to keep all that I commanded you,
wha ana 'ammkon-na kullhon yawmata
And behold, I am with you all the days
'adamma lSulameh d'alma.
until the end of the world.

187

At the sea of Tiberias

J21,5-25

Tlaye lma it lkon middem lmil'as?
Children, have you anything to eat?
armaw mciddtekon mingabba dyammina daspitta
Cast the net to the right side of the boat
wmiSkxin-tton:
and you will find some.
ayttau min nune dcadton haSa.
Bring some of the fish that you have just caught.
tau iStarrau!
Come, have breakfast!
Sim'on bar yona raxem att li yattir min halen?
Simon son of John, do you love me more than these?
r'i li imrai.
Feed my lambs.
Sim'on bar yona raxem att li?
Simon son of John, do you love me?
r'l li 'irbai.
Tend my sheep.
Sim'on bar yona raxem att li?
Simon son of John, do you love me?
r'l li nqawati.
Feed my sheep.
amen amen amar-na lak dkad Tle wait
Truly, truly I tell you, when you were young,
att lnapSak asar wait xaccaik
you used to dress yourself
wamhallek wait laika dcabe att:
and go where you wished,
ma den dasebet tlpSoT idaik
but when you grow old, you will stretch out your hands
waxren yesor lak xaccaik wyawblak
and another will dress you and lead you
laika dla cabe att:
where you do not wish to go.
ta batari!
Follow me!
in cabe-na daiqawwe hana 'adamma date-na lak ma lak?
If it is my will that he remain until I come, what is that to you?
att ta batari!
You follow me!

The Last Words before the Ascension
L24,44-50 Acts1,4-8

halen innen mille dmallet 'ammkon kad lwatkon weit:
These are my words that I spoke to you while I was with you,
dwale-w diSttallam koll middem daktib boraita dmuSe
that everything must be fulfilled written in the law of Moses,
wbanbiyye wabmazmore 'alai:
and in the prophets, and in the psalms about me.
dhakanna ktib whakanna zadeq wa dyexxaS mSixa:
For so it is written that was right for the Messiah to suffer
wdaiqum min beit mite latlata yawmin:
and rise from the dead on the third day, and
waditkrez baSmeh tyabuta lSubqana
to be preached in his name the repentance for forgiveness
daxaTahe bkullhon 'amme: wSurraya ihwe min oriSlem.
of sins to all the nations, beginning from Jerusalem.
atton innon sahadde dhalen.
You are witnesses of these things.
wana eSaddar 'alaikon mulkana dabi:
And I am sending upon you the Promise of my Father;
atton den qawwau boriSlem mditta
but you stay in the city of Jerusalem
'adamma dtilbSun xaila min rawma.
until you have been clothed with power from on high.
haw daSma'ton menni:
This is what you have heard from me;
dyoxannan a'med bmaiya
for John baptized with water,
watton te'imdun bruxa dqudSa
but you will be baptized with the Holy Spirit
la batar yawmata saggiye.
not many days from now.
la wat dilkon hade lmedda' zabna aw zabne
It is not for you to know the times or seasons
ailen daba sam innon bSulTana dnapSeh:
that the Father has set by his own authority.
ella kad tete ruxa dqudSa 'alaikon
but when the Holy Spirit comes upon you,
tqabblun xaila:
you will receive power,
wtihwon li sahadde boriSlem wabkullah ihud
and you will be my witnesses in Jerusalem and in all Judea
wap beit Samraye w'adamma lsawppeh dar'a.
and Samaria, and to the ends of the earth.

THE SECOND COMING

Rev22,12-20

ha ate-na 'agal wagri 'ammi:
See, I am coming soon and my reward is with me,
lmipra' lkoll xad ak ditawhi 'abadeh.
to repay according to everyone's work.
ana-na alap wtaw:
I am the Alpha and the Omega,
qadmaya waxraya: reSa wSulama.
the First and the Last, the Beginning and the End.
en ate-na 'agal.
Yes, I am coming soon.

* * * * *

THE CHRISTIAN PRAYER

Rev22,17-20 1Cor16,22

wruxa wkallta amrin: ta.
And the Spirit and the bride say, 'Come.'
wman dSama' yemar: ta
And let everyone who hears say, 'Come.'
wman dache yete.
And let everyone who is thirsty come.
wman dcabe issab maiya xaiye maggan.
Let anyone who wishes take the water of life freely.
amen ta marya yeSu'!
Amen. Come Lord Jesus!
marana ta!
Our Lord, come!

* * * * *

SOURCES

Biblia Hebraica Stuttgartensia, 1997
Biblia Sacra Vulgata, 1994
Nestle-Aland , *Novum Testamentum Graece et Latine* 1997
The New Testament, Peshitta Text, Mosul-Bagdad, 1950
Syriac NT and Psalms, Istambul, 1994
Syriac Bible, Syrian Patriarchate,1996
Crawford Burkitt, *Evangelion Da-Mepharreshe,* Cambridge 1904 *The New Covenant, Peshitta Aramaic Text,* Jerusalem, 1986
Kurt Aland, *Synopsis Quattuor Evangeliorum,* 1997
G.Dalman, *Grammatik des Judisch-Palastinischen Aramaisch,*1894
G.Dalman, *Worte Jesu,*1898
Burney, *The Poetry of our Lord,* Oxford
Kohlenberger, *The Precise Parallel New Testament,* Oxford 1989
Errico, *The Message of Matthew,*1996
Black, *An Aramaic Approach to the Gospels and Acts,* 1967
Payne Smith, *Thesaurus Syriacus,*1999
William Jennings, *Lexicon to the Syriac New Testament,* Oxord 1926
Bover, *Evangeliorum Concordia,* 1943
Stevenson, *Palestinian Jewish Aramaic,*1999
Strack, *Grammatik des Biblisch-Aramaischen,*1921
Noeldeke T, *Syriac Grammar,* 2001
Thackston Wheeler, *Introduction to Syriac,* 1999
George Kiraz, *Comparative Edition of the Syriac Gospels,* 1996
George Kiraz, *The Syriac Primer,* 2001
George Kiraz, *Lexical Tools to the Syriac New Testament, 1994*
Dom Palacios, *Grammatica Syriaca,* 1931

LaVergne, TN USA
30 June 2010
187901LV00002B/78/A

9 781581 126044